EVALUATION
in the BASIC COLLEGE

EVALUATION
in the BASIC COLLEGE

AT MICHIGAN STATE UNIVERSITY

Edited by Paul L. Dressel

Director of Evaluation Services, Michigan State University

HARPER & BROTHERS, PUBLISHERS, NEW YORK

CONTENTS

PREFACE

In the early stages of the planning of this volume, one title considered was *So Little We Know*. Regretfully discarded as inexplicit, the phrase is still an apt description of the spirit in which the book was written. Nevertheless, in the years since the Basic College was founded and the Office of Evaluation Services (formerly the Board of Examiners) was established, some knowledge about the program has been accumulated and this knowledge has, in turn, played some part in influencing the views of those associated with the program. I hope the results recorded here—which represent only a part of what has been done—will interest others.

It is the process rather than the results which are important, however, for such studies as those reported here are never really done. As a program is modified, partly perhaps because of the evidence accumulated, new studies must be undertaken. The results found in one institution may not hold in another. We hope this report of continuing activity will encourage others to similar studies. Educational planning on the basis of a little knowledge is laden with error, but with continuing evaluation it can be self-corrective.

The development of this volume has been an unusually interesting experience. As the first and only director of the office which has been largely concerned with the studies reported herein, I have been closely associated with all the contributors and have been aware of, if not actually involved in, all of the studies mentioned as they were in process. Accordingly, the editorial work has in the fullest sense been a labor of love with an occasional nostalgic remembrance added.

The Basic College has been fortunate in having a succession of able deans: Howard C. Rather, now deceased; Clifford E. Erickson, now Dean of the College of Education, M.S.U.; Thomas H. Hamilton, now Vice President for Academic Affairs, M.S.U.; and Edward A. Carlin, the current dean, a contributor to this volume. Each of these men in turn has taken an active interest in evaluation and given every possible encouragement and assistance to educational research. The department heads in the Basic College have always been interested and helpful. Particularly is this true of Paul D. Bagwell, Communication Skills; Chester A. Lawson, Natural Science; Walter R. Fee, Social Science; and Harry Kimber, Humanities—all of whom have headed Basic College departments since 1944. My associates and I are appreciative of the help and suggestions for studies received from all of these persons.

My own conception of evaluation has developed largely out of association with the work of Ralph W. Tyler. Many of the ideas in Chapter 2 have been previously expressed by him. Although it was written without direct reference to any of his writings it is not impossible that I may even have used exact phrases of his. If so, it will not only confirm my respect for his views but also for his clear and concise expression of them.

I wish to express my appreciation to the contributors to this volume. Both in the quality of their work and in their enthusiasm in writing about it, they have made the task as editor a pleasurable one. My secretary, Ruth A. Frye, has also contributed greatly to bringing this volume into final form.

East Lansing, Michigan   Paul L. Dressel
March 1958

Part I

ABOUT
EVALUATION

1

PAUL L. DRESSEL

So Little We Know

The Shifting Scene in the Ongoing Drama

Using modern high-speed photography it is possible, in effect, to
stop a bullet at any point in flight, including the instant of impact. It is then possible to examine in detail and with accuracy
what is happening to the bullet and to the object upon which it
has its final impact.

The individual engaged in educational research sometimes
wishes that the educational process would behave as predictably
as the bullet and that he had the means to study education in
process and in impact with as much detail and accuracy. Education is a variable made up of many other variables. A changing
student body, a changing instructional staff, new materials, new
administrators, and shifting pressures from governing bodies and
public sources often result in a program of educational research
being set up in one context and ending in a different one. But
even in his frustration at the changing nature of what he is trying to study, no evaluator would wish to replace that condition
of flux by one of sterile stability.

According to the Heisenberg Uncertainty Principle, it is impossible to measure at the same time the position and the velocity of a particle. In measuring the position of a particle any
technique used changes the velocity. On the other hand, an experiment designed to measure velocity cannot yield exact information about position. Although there is doubt among

3

scientists as to the applicability of the Heisenberg Uncertainty Principle to macroscopic phenomena, the idea has analogous use in education and the study of the educational process. At any point in time the individual student is exposed to many different educational experiences. Each individual has a different selection of experiences from every other one, if for no other reason than that he perceives the experience in a different way due to his own past experiences. Any attempt to study an individual requires a collection of data by a variety of means to the point where the individual's educational experiences actually are modified by the study. His perception of them may be changed even more. Even the attempt to study the educational process on a less intensive basis changes the process. A few years ago, in visiting for a few weeks the class of an able and experienced teacher, I was impressed with this teacher's repeated remark that the class atmosphere was considerably changed by my presence.

If we turn to the measurement of changes in individuals over a period of time, several difficulties arise. The teacher of a course would like to know the effect of that particular course among all the other influences operating upon the individual during the period of months or years under study. The interaction and the composite effect of the variety of experiences, however, make it impossible to determine where an individual developed the qualities that he has at the end of the period. We can observe gross changes; we cannot say with any certainty how those changes came about.

We are indeed caught in the dilemma of the uncertainty principle. If at a specific point in time or with one individual we attempt to study in detail the educational process, we change the process and the effect of the process. If we concentrate on the measurement of gross changes over a period of time, we are unable to say at what point or in what sequence the changes came about.

Most of the studies and speculations reported here were carried on at Michigan State University during the period 1944–1955. This period has been one of rapid growth in student body, physical facilities, and services. It has also been a period of reorganization—facetiously dramatized in the remark of one faculty member that he had developed the habit of stopping by the dean's office each morning to find out who his department head was before going on to his office. If the changes had been as rapid and as irrational as the humorous remark implied, the educational researcher could do little but throw up his hands in despair and quit. One who attempts to be rational in an irrational environment is either crazy already or will be shortly. The extensive changes with which we have had to cope were in general based upon reasonable and demanding considerations with which the researchers were usually in sympathy, however much they might be chagrined because of the effect on their own plans.

Without attempting to detail developments which have been more adequately reported elsewhere, it does seem worthwhile and even necessary to describe a little of the over-all situation in which the studies here reported were conducted and to indicate some of the major changes in this situation over the period covered.

IN THE BASIC COLLEGE

The Basic College was organized in 1944, instruction in the Basic courses beginning in the fall of that year. The Basic College was and is an administrative unit providing a program of general education required of all students in the University. In the original program there were seven courses: Written and Spoken English, required of all students; Physical Science and Biological Science, one of these to be taken by each student; Social Science and Effective Living, one of these to be taken by each student; History of Civilization and Literature and Fine Arts, one of this pair to be taken by each student. The student also was required to take one additional Basic course beyond the four thus specified, to make a total of 45 quarter hours.

These requirements accounted for approximately one-fourth of his total college degree program and approximately 50 per cent of his first two years' work.

This program was subject to attack on a number of grounds:

1. Those individuals rightfully concerned about the preparation of their major students looked at the block of time assigned to the Basic courses with longing eyes and, of course, noted that the requirement of the fifth course called for a double sampling in one of the areas of paired courses, whereas in the other two a single course was deemed adequate. A natural suggestion was that the requirement be reduced.

2. The possibility of considering the total Basic College requirements as a program of general education was practically eliminated by the fact that an instructor faced with a given group of students could not know with any certainty just what pattern of general education courses they might be taking.

3. Since the choice among alternatives tended to be dictated by the curriculum selected, the original intent that students might elect among the alternatives to broaden their experience was lost.

4. Finally, for various reasons, three of the original seven courses came under very critical scrutiny by faculty and students. For example, the physical science area was not attractive to students and, in addition, the possibility of taking it was ruled out by many of the curricula.

The need for some major change was indicated. In the fall of 1953 a revised program was put in effect.

The considerations just discussed indicated that the four courses—Communication Skills, Natural Science, Social Science, and Humanities—to be required of all students should replace the original seven. This decision, thoughtfully arrived at, was put into effect with what in retrospect seems undue speed, causing some resulting morale problems and difficulties not entirely eliminated two years later. Indeed the difficulties of planning broad courses of the general education type are not to be minimized. The possible selection of materials is so wide and the possible approaches so numerous that consensus is difficult to achieve in a large staff. Changing views of individuals and staff turnover make course change from year to year a thing to be expected. Seldom has any one of the courses been the same for two years in succession.

IN THE EVALUATION SERVICES

When the Basic College was organized, there was also introduced a Board of Examiners, placed originally in the Dean of Students' Office but given major functions in connection with the new general education program. This Board was charged with the preparation—in cooperation with the various departments—of comprehensive examinations used to determine the final grade of the student in each course. In this program the student received from the instructor a temporary grade for each of the three terms of the course and then took a final comprehensive examination which resulted in a single grade for the entire course. Provision was made for the granting of special permission to take the examination early and receive full credit, provided a C or higher grade was obtained. Grades were determined from standards based on the work of regularly enrolled students. The Board was also charged, although less formally, with the responsibility of carrying on some studies of the general education program and of organizing a pre-testing program to be used in the variety of decisions with regard to the placement and acceleration of students.

Such separation of the examining and grading functions was a novelty which could not but attract attention and generate resistance. The acceleration program also excited some distaste, with some people feeling that the C grade was not an adequate standard for granting credit and others questioning whether the granting of credit by examination was really a respectable academic procedure. While originally the independence of the Board of Examiners from the Basic College was seen as a safeguard of its freedom to develop good and comprehensive examinations, this independence also became a target for criticism. Accordingly, about the time when the course revision mentioned earlier was put into effect, changes were made in the Board of Examiners and the examination program to tie the examinations and the instruction closer together. More use was made of dual appointees between the instructional department and the Board, although the chief examiner in each area continued to be a full-time appointee of the Board of Examiners.

The comprehensive examination was reduced from a program of examinations covering all three terms of a course to separate examinations for each term of the course. The student's final grade in each term now became a 50–50 composite of an instructor's grade and an examination grade. Unfavorable reactions to the name, as well as its lack of descriptiveness of function, led to a change of name from Board of Examiners to Office of Evaluation Services. These changes seem to have met most of the criticisms. Such dissatisfactions as continue to exist are probably inevitable concomitants of any required program of examinations.

IN THE COUNSELING CENTER

Recognizing that a larger percentage of students were coming to the University with uncertainty about what field of specialization or what vocation they ultimately wished to enter, the Basic College program was regarded as providing an opportunity for exploration. The applicability of basic courses to all majors and the possible deferment of a choice of major provided by a no-preference admission combined to increase further the number of students who either did not make a choice initially or who changed their minds. Coincidentally with the introduction of the Basic College, therefore, a Counseling Center staffed with professional counselors was established. This department is administratively in the Dean of Students' Office but is closely coordinated with the Basic College program in a number of respects.

During the first two years, all students are dually enrolled in the Basic College and the college of their preferred major as of time of entry. However, the preferred majors may be changed at any time during the first two years by obtaining the permission of the Dean of the Basic College. The policy was adopted that all preference changes should be initiated by going to the Counseling Center. In most cases, after the preference change is initiated by the Counseling Center, the approval by the Dean's Office is automatic. The Counseling Center has also given special attention to those students completely undecided about a major. For several years the counselors acted as advisers for all so-called "no-preference" students. In more recent years, the Basic College faculty has assumed this responsibility and fortunately so, because the numbers became too great for the Counseling Center to handle. The Counseling Center also serves as an auxiliary to the Dean's Office in working with students in scholastic difficulty. More recently, the Counseling staff has also had considerable interest in the able students and has collaborated with the Basic College in this regard.

IN THE UNIVERSITY

The initiation of the Basic College required a major administrative alteration and was accompanied by a reorganization of what we frequently call the "upper colleges." During this period, also, new departments and new colleges have been added, and functions and responsibilities have been reassigned. Most of these changes were of minor significance to the studies reported here, for most of these studies are related to the program of the first two years. However, the shifting of the majors in physical education from the College of Business and Public Service to the College of Education illustrates the kind of reorganization that causes difficulty in studies involving data by colleges and by curricula within the colleges. Since the physical education group is academically one of the less able ones, the shifting of this group from one college to another makes considerable difference in the statistics from that point on. Changing the coding in a set of IBM cards, or finding a place for a new coding when changes make this necessary can be a difficult and irritating experience.

The Interrogative Phase

WHO WANTS TO KNOW WHAT?

Most educational research results from a question. The nature and the specificity of the questions raised vary. So, too, does the urgency with which the questions are to be answered. Perhaps the most troublesome issue in the carrying through of studies is that they are too frequently undertaken as a result of a biased question. Thus, the individual who raises a question as to what students think of the objective examinations has perhaps reached a conclusion in his own mind that objective examinations are unsatisfactory. If the results contradict the point of view which he has unconsciously adopted, his tendency is to rationalize the evidence. One easy way out is to argue that the researcher is biased in favor of objective examinations and has, therefore, interpreted these results in a way not justified by the facts of the situation.

Again, the biased questioner may weigh the results differently from the way the investigator had in mind. If the initial question implies that admission standards are too high, thereby eliminating many individuals who might successfully complete college, there can be an honest difference of opinion about the meaning of an investigation which shows that lowering the admission standards to include a less able group yields only one graduate for every fifty so admitted. In such cases the questioner may point to the one in fifty as proving his case, whereas others may reach the opposite conclusion. It is difficult for a researcher to keep his own value judgments from entering into his remarks.

There will always be disagreement as to what type of effort

should be dignified by the title "research." Much of what is reported in this volume could be appropriately labelled "service studies." Without getting involved in fine points of definition, one possible difference between a service study and a research study involves the nature of the question asked in the first place. A service study involves the study of a problem arising in a practical situation; the question originally raised is stated in relationship to some ongoing function. The very raising of the question also implies less than complete satisfaction with the existing way of handling the function. This implication can cause some difficulty in making an objective study and so interpreting it that the values and biases of the researcher do not enter into the picture.

To admit that a particular practice may not be the best one is sufficient grounds for justifying a study of the practice, but it does not mean that a better practice exists. Usually, however, it is only when someone has doubts about present practice and some idea of a possible change that a question is raised. Thus the raising of the question almost inevitably arouses anxiety in others who see in this question evidence of dissatisfaction with their present activity. Moreover the questions are frequently raised by administrative superiors or associates of those involved in an activity rather than by those responsible for the activity. It is usually easier for a person outside the situation to be objective and critical, to raise questions, and to wonder whether there isn't a better way of doing a job. It is often the administrators who worry about improvement of teaching rather than the teachers. The faculty is more inclined to fuss about admission practices than is the admissions officer.

FOOLS ASK QUESTIONS

The adage that "fools ask questions which wise men can't answer" might almost as truthfully be rephrased as "wise men ask questions which only fools can answer." To ask a meaningful question requires that one understand the fundamental nature of the problem about which the question is raised. The individual who raises a question as to what per cent of a class should fail understands little of the nature of the grading process. No answer, including the answer that there is no answer, will be satisfactory to that individual until his grasp of the whole problem of judging the achievement of other individuals becomes much more perceptive.

The individual who asks for assistance in defining a minimum set of standards in knowledge, skills, and abilities demonstrates thereby a deeper level of understanding; so does the individual who simply raises a question about the actual practice in this institution and this department as to the percentage of students failed. Both of the last two questions are answerable—in contrast to the unanswerable question of the first worrier about grades. Without some insight into a problem it is not possible to raise sensible questions.

PERPETUAL IRRESOLVABLE ISSUES

A great deal of time is spent in studying problems or issues for which there is no really good solution. There probably is no final answer for any significant question about education, since education is a social institution. Education will mean different things, therefore, in different times and places. The irresolvability of certain issues, however, is due not so much to the relativity of the answers as it is to the breadth of the questions themselves. When an individual asks "How many students should fail this course?" it is impossible to give the general answer he expects. With Instructor A teaching this course to certain kinds of students in a certain type of institution it may be possible to make some reasonable assumptions which will yield an answer. Another question raised continually over a long period of years has to do with the matter of class size. Are small classes more effective than large classes? As phrased, this question has no answer.

We are too prone to phrase questions in a way that indicates expectation of an answer in the form of some broad principle or law which has few exceptions. Most things are more complicated than they seem to many people. The effect of class size is tied in with the objectives of instruction, the type of classroom available, the kind of students involved, the teaching methods used, and the abilities and personal qualities of the particular instructor. Phrased in terms of these factors, the subject becomes sensitive and interest in the answer fades, for one soon finds that the academic profession has its taboos. One of these is not to raise questions about the relative teaching efficiency of individuals. No study of class size is reported in this volume.

There are, then, perpetual and irresolvable issues of two types. In one case the answer is relative, temporary, and subject to changing conditions. In the other case, the arbitrary limitations which we impose—the taboos about which one must not raise questions—so circumscribe the issue that it is impossible to deal with it in a way which would yield any really significant answer. Even if some of these complex issues were opened up on the most fundamental basis there is no assurance that any meaningful answer would be arrived at. There can be no useful answer provided for the question at such a level of generality as: "Are small classes more effective than large ones?"

The Difficulties of the Declarative

THE MISSING PERSONS

The presentation of unclear or impossible questions is not the only difficulty in making studies of an ongoing educational program. In our experience there have always been more questions waiting for answers than we were able to come to grips with. In the early years of the Basic College, a sizeable number of the Basic College faculty were candidates for the doctorate and under the necessity of finding a dissertation project. A few of the projects touched upon in this volume were carried out as dissertations or were follow-ups of some work initiated in a dissertation. In retrospect, also, it seems as though in the earlier years the staffs of the various courses were more desirous of collecting evidence which would help them in making some of their decisions. With the accumulation of experience, with the increasing pressures due to enrollment, and with few people under the necessity of carrying out a project for dissertation purposes, the amount of educational research done by instructional staff members has tended to decrease markedly.

Two additional factors would appear to contribute to this, although they would be perhaps hard to substantiate. Educational research activity has not the status that more traditional types of research have in the special fields. In the pressure for achievement of academic respectability there has perhaps been a tendency to avoid educational research studies in favor of other types of research. Discussion with some of the individuals who earlier carried on evaluation and research studies suggests that in some cases the failure of these studies to yield definitive results caused the individual and his associates to question the value of continued activity of that kind. Some of the individuals reporting studies in this volume failed to carry the studies as far as they had hoped because of such experiences.

Added to this, there has always been some hesitancy about experimental situations which required modification of usual practice. The individual who wished to treat certain sections of a class differently from others, to select certain types of students for special treatment, or to keep the same group of students together over more than one quarter always found some difficulty in making arrangements of this sort. Seldom was any proposal involving this kind of thing dismissed as impossible; but evident lack of enthusiasm on the part of an administrator quickly cools the ardor of the neophyte researcher.

With this complication of factors we have increasingly faced the problem of the missing persons. An attempt has been made to correct this situation through providing in the Office of Evaluation Services some time for research and for consultation with others on research. Most of the studies reported in this volume involved some member of the Office of Evaluation Services, either in an active or in an advisory capacity. In fact, this was a major consideration in selecting the studies to be reviewed here. Another source of researchers has been found in doctoral candidates, other than Basic College staff members, from the College of Education. Several significant studies were undertaken and completed by such persons. The Office has also made occasional use of some part-time appointments of graduate students working on the doctorate, and has maintained one so-called "floating position" which is assigned each year to a different instructional department of the Basic College. This provides opportunity for some individual to carry out a study of significance to him and to his department. In such fashion we have kept things moving, but always with a feeling that there were many more things to be done and that those that were being done were proceeding too slowly. So it is that we often remark that "this would be a good thing to do if we could only find the person to do it."

TEMPUS FUGIT AND PEOPLE FIDGET

With few exceptions, significant research takes time—time in planning, execution, analyzing data, and writing up results. In the study of changes in students, considerable time must elapse before one can complete the project. In a project of the magnitude of the one carried on in the social science course—a part of which is reported in Chapter 3 by Carlin—many hours of his time and that of others in the department was spent in the late summer and early fall of 1954 laying out their plans for the project. Following this there was an interval of unavoidable inactivity wherein the students completed one, two, and three terms of social science, with further collection of evidence at the end of each term. The maintenance of enthusiasm for a project extending over a period of time is difficult.

When questions are once raised there is an interest at the moment in knowing what the answer is. After the lapse of some months even the specific meaning of the question itself may be forgotten by those other than the person actively engaged in the research—and the question may well have changed its meaning for him. In the Carlin project the total amount of data collected was such as to necessitate punched card procedures involving a considerable amount of assistance from statisticians and tabulating machine operators. The result is that two years after the project was initiated there is still little in the way of a report. Unquestionably the impact of the study is thereby reduced.

Fleeting time and fidgeting people enter into the research problem in other ways. A few years ago, when we planned a follow-up of our new graduates' reactions to the general education courses, we ran into the difficulty that by the time the project was completed and the reactions of a group of seniors obtained the decision had been made to change to a new program of basic courses. The result was that when the senior reactions were tabulated, summarized, and interpreted, the evidence applied to an old program with which the faculty was no longer concerned.

Apparently simple questions also may involve time elements which are hardly understood by the interested questioner. A question such as that of how the ability of students at the present time compares with that of students in the institution ten or twenty years ago ought to have an immediate and simple answer. In fact, of course, one cannot go further back than the time when a testing program was used on all students. Even so, questions about the shifting meaning of a test and the problem of equating instruments now used with those of an earlier period are not easily resolvable except as one works out a program to obtain extensive statistical results. In the case of this question, at least a year and a half elapsed before anything like an answer could be provided and then it was not entirely unambiguous.

THE DIFFERENCE BETWEEN MAY AND MIGHT

The nature of educational research studies of the type reported here and the role of a person carrying out those studies is often not fully understood by the researcher himself and even more frequently not understood by the potential consumers of the results.

To use an analogy, in historical research it is now an accepted point of view that each generation must interpret or reinterpret history for itself. The accrual of additional evidence and the trends of development since the last interpretation may result in a different point of view about a specific historical event or period.

Similarly, in educational research the day will never come when it will be possible to say unequivocally and for all time that any particular educational procedure will attain such and such results for all individuals. The results of a study simply provide additional insights into the problem. It may provide evidence which tends to reject certain points of view about a problem and which is more or less consistent with certain other points of view. The final judgment, however, involves values and often involves placing a priority on values. If lowering admission standards yields only one successful graduate out of every five hundred additional people admitted, the decision as to whether or not admission standards should be lowered depends on which of several considerations is placed foremost.

The administrator who wields the might would like definite answers. Occasionally there is one who only wants evidence to justify what he intends to do anyway. The researcher deals in probabilities and assumptions. If he permits his values to enter into the stating of definite courses of action he should realize himself and he should make clear to all others concerned that his recommendations are not solely the result of the research. Seldom can a researcher provide clear single-valued answers to the questions which others want answered.

In All Humility

Our title suggests a reviewing, on the basis of some of the objective evidence available, of the changes in our educational program over a period of years. Our injunction to each of the writers has been to cover the variety of studies of the topic covered by his chapter, and then sum up accumulated studies in the perspective which he obtained in the process of reviewing them. The task thus undertaken is really an evaluation and an interpretation of the significance of our accumulated efforts. We hope the effort will yield more than just a review or repetition of numerous studies—many of which assume meaning only in relationship to other studies.

We hope to present a picture which will be of interest to that large group of college administrators and faculty members who have in recent years become concerned with self studies and educational research adventures. We hope further through this review to see more clearly the meaning and the weaknesses of our past efforts and thereby to plan more intelligently for the future. If we achieve only the latter of these two hopes, we shall be satisfied. If we also provide some impetus to educational studies —although in full realization of the fact that they do not provide definite answers—we shall be more than satisfied.

2

PAUL L. DRESSEL

Curriculum Planning

Evaluation is Inevitable

The issue is not whether an educational program is to be evaluated; rather, it is simply a matter of the kind of evidence used in doing it. Prejudice is a great time-saver, for it enables us to make judgments without bothering to collect evidence. But in the long run, judgments made on the basis of relevant evidence are more valid than subjective emotional reactions. Yet beyond the objective evidence, no matter how extensive it may be, are values and practical considerations which must color judgments.

Conceivably through the use of new and expensive equipment (closed circuit television, perhaps) some significant advance could be achieved in the mastery of certain skills. Limited funds enforce a choice, and the decision as to whether the amount of improvement justifies the financial expenditure involves values which transcend the objective evidence. Administrators and teachers may not reach the same conclusion. Evaluation, then, includes both the accumulation and organization of relevant evidence and the weighing and relating of this evidence to other considerations in an attempt to reach an actual decision.

In the following chapters an attempt is made to portray both aspects of evaluation. In Chapter 7 by Jackson, for example, is reported a study of that phase of our admissions program which was based upon test results. The final action taken in modifying the admissions program was based upon factors largely irrelevant to the research. Nevertheless, the experiences and the favorable results of the research project yielded the insights which led to a different program. The later study by Matteson reported in Chapter 12 indicated that it was, indeed, an improved procedure.

The results of the studies reported in this volume are intrinsic to Michigan State. And yet they have implications for other programs even though the specific findings may be different for other institutions. This chapter clarifies this significance by suggesting the possible contributions of evaluation to the steps of curriculum planning and at the same time indicating the relations of the studies reported in later chapters to the discussion. Thus the significance of such studies may become more apparent, even though the conditions at Michigan State limit the applicability of the results.

Evaluation is Helpful

IN SELECTING OBJECTIVES

Education effects changes in behavior. These desired changes in behavior are stated as objectives. There are, of course, many ways in which students may change: increased knowledge, new ideas, new skills, broader and more intensive interests. If education is effective, students think differently. Such desirable objectives can be extended almost endlessly. However, the time for formal education is limited and it is necessary to identify the most important changes which formal education can produce so that these rather than less important goals may become the guides for curriculum planning. The objectives of a curriculum are matters of choice. Yet this conscious choice often is supplanted by deference to tradition and authority or becomes only an uncritical acceptance of existing practice. This is unfortunate, for there are sources of information relevant to the choice of objectives and these should be explored before making the choice.

First of all, we should know something about the students we have to teach: their present knowledge, their interests, their problems, and their deficiencies. The answers will vary from college to college and may suggest somewhat different objectives or a different order of priority with regard to objectives. The four chapters of Part II represent attempts at Michigan State to find out something about our students: their backgrounds, their reasons for dropping out, and something of their interests and their reactions.

A second consideration in choosing objectives should be contemporary life. We need to familiarize ourselves with the opportunities and the demands placed upon individuals by our contemporary society. The ever-present threat of atomic warfare suggests the need for attention to the social implications of science as much as it does to the study of the nature of fission and fusion. The rate at which new developments appear in medicine and technology and in all branches of knowledge suggests that developing interest in and reading to keep abreast of these developments may be an objective of prime importance. There also is evidence that emphasis on the sciences to the virtual exclusion of the humanities from some curricula is a matter which demands immediate correction. Such an analysis of contemporary life is a form of research or evaluation. Little of such research is reported in this volume, although Carlin's discussion in Chapter 3 of the increasing importance attached to graduate level education touches upon it. On the whole, however, the analysis of the problems and demands of contemporary life as a basis for defining educational objectives has developed out of the knowledge and experience of the instructional staff.

A third source of information for the definition and selection of educational objectives is found in the recommendations of specialists in the subject matter and professional fields. For example, various medical and engineering groups have made pronouncements as to the importance of a strong general education component in training for their respective fields. The recommendations of specialists run the gamut from explicit formulation of the facts that students should know to statements of general objectives involving abilities, attitudes, and personality traits. Researchers in the area of science education, for example, have undertaken to define general principles which emphasize the significance of educational objectives involving understanding and application in contrast with rote memorization and definition. In general education, college professors tend to be their own preferred specialists. Nevertheless, some of the studies in this book are attempts to agree upon or to clarify objectives.

The usual, although not always recognized, dilemma in the process of selecting and defining objectives is that the resulting list is too long for any teacher to keep in mind. Some basis must be found for selecting those which are most important, to which adequate attention can be given, and toward which students can make some significant progress. Indeed, this choice is what makes the formulation of objectives exceedingly important. There are many worthwhile things to do and some choice is necessary. Having too many objectives is just as dangerous as having none.

Some reduction in number of objectives may be achieved by grouping them. For example, persons concerned with the objective of critical thinking have elaborated it into fifty and even more subobjectives. Some of these are only matters of choice in wording. The attempt to clarify objectives may also bring out the fact that many verbal distinctions have no counterpart in human behavior. Thus the attempts to evaluate student achievement in regard to the objective leads to rephrasing the objective to correspond more with actual human behavior and the kinds of judgments that can be made of it. Palmer's discussions, in Chapter 8, of the problems of judging written and oral work illustrate this situation. The experiences in attempting to evaluate critical thinking as reported in Chapter 13 led similarly to the conclusion that not more than five or six aspects of critical thinking were distinguishable.

Two sets of criteria are to be utilized in selecting those goals which are to be given priority. The first of these is the educational and social philosophy of the school. For example, if the ideal society is regarded as one made up of men who can and will make their own decisions and who meet and solve their own problems rather than blindly obeying authority, then critical thinking or problem solving will be given priority over certain other objectives. Screening objectives for their importance in reference to the accepted educational philosophy insures that from the objectives originally chosen in part by study of contemporary life, we will choose those which mirror our hopes of the good life and good society of the future.

In the following chapters little is said that bears explicitly on the role of an educational philosophy in choice of objectives, although an educational philosophy may be implied by the emphasis on certain objectives. However, as many of the chapters make clear, there is no single accepted educational philosophy in the Basic College program. As Mayhew points out in Chapter 14, objectives involving attitudes have always been important, but the staff has disagreed as to the importance of these objectives. Where different points of view exist, a statement of objectives may become a circus tent under which diverse points of view are accommodated with each group seeking that ring which appeals to its fancy. If the alternative of striving for a statement of objectives which represents the minimum acceptable to all points of view is chosen, the objectives may be little more than statements of the content to be covered in each course. Under these circumstances, evaluation may help to restore objectives to their proper role.

The second set of criteria for the selection of important objectives is to be found in what is known of the nature of learning. There is little point to listing as course objectives behavioral changes which are impossible of attainment or which are appropriately assignable to other agencies, courses, or grade levels. For example, our Basic courses serve a recognized function in orienting students to the major fields of knowledge, but assistance in vocational planning is regarded as more effectively supplied by the Counseling Center and by representatives of the various specialized curricula. There are also psychological studies which indicate that learning proceeds best when:

1. The student is motivated to learn through grasping the purpose of learning and the relationship to his own needs of what is to be learned.

2. There is a relationship between what is to be learned and the previous experience of the student.

3. When the student is an active contributor rather than a passive recipient.

4. When the material learned is shortly used or applied in dealing with other materials or problems.

Those objectives which, for students of a given maturity and background, promise greater achievement because they permit capitalizing on these principles, may appropriately be given more attention than others. Objectives which require the learning of specific unrelated facts, names, dates, and the like, do not ordinarily take advantage of these principles of learning.

IN PLANNING LEARNING EXPERIENCES

The second stage in curriculum development requires the planning of learning experiences. The components of a curriculum are essentially three in number. One of these involves the materials of instruction: subject matter or content, books, films, and other equipment available for use by the teacher and student. The second component includes the methods of instruction such as lecture, discussion, laboratory, individual projects, and the like. The third component is made up of the learning activities of the student which may vary from passive absorption of impressions from the teacher and text to active mental and physical participation in planning, carrying out, and interpreting of projects and experiments. These interrelated components of the curriculum—materials, methods, and student activities—make up the educational experiences by means of which we hope to achieve the agreed-upon objectives. Logically, the experiences are to be chosen in relation to the objectives.

Logically too, the learning experiences provided cannot differ in any essential way from the situations which we use to evaluate student progress relative to the objectives. If the objectives are confined to knowledge, there is no difficulty either in selection of educational experiences or in evaluation. The facts are covered and the students are tested for their knowledge of them. For objectives involving intellectual abilities and affective outcomes, the selection of learning experiences is more difficult. Here evaluation can make a contribution.

The first task of evaluation is that of determining what an objective means in behavioral terms. What does an individual do which enables us to observe or infer that he is progressing in the direction implied by an objective? The experiences of Palmer and Nelson reported in Chapter 8 provide some indication of how work on examinations provides insights on the effectiveness or ineffectiveness of certain experiences. Some of the experimentation with various instructional techniques mentioned in Chapters 13 and 14 also exemplify the contribution of evaluation to making decisions about the worth of types of educational experiences.

Still another example of the contribution of evaluation to the selection of learning experiences is found in the repeated occasions when our examiners found that a carefully worked out exercise was rendered invalid for further use in testing because one or more instructors thought it so appropriate that it was taken over for classroom use. This emphasizes again that good evaluation requires clarification of objectives and the development of situations wherein the student's capabilities in regard to the objective can be brought in evidence. Evaluation, therefore, should be useful in suggesting appropriate learning experiences.

In selecting textual materials, studies of the reading level of these materials have been made. Student reactions to materials, methods, and activities have also been collected as a basis for selecting or revising courses. Such studies are usually limited in nature, directed to a definite decision, and hence of little or no interest after that decision is reached.

IN ORGANIZING LEARNING EXPERIENCES

The third step in the planning of a curriculum is the organization of learning experiences for maximum achievement of the objectives. The important outcomes of education are not achievable in the limited periods of time corresponding to a quarter or even to a single course extending over three quarters. A single learning experience may show little effect, but if experiences are so planned as to reinforce preceding ones, the cumulative effect can produce marked changes.

A cumulative organization should possess three characteristics. First, there must be planned repetition whereby a variety of experiences at intervals confront the student with major elements which he is expected to learn. Second, these experiences should develop deeper and broader insight. The continuity in elements implied by the first characteristic should be coupled with a sequential development such that the later learning experiences build on and add to the earlier ones. Finally, the experiences in any one course should be related to other courses and to activities and problems outside the classroom.

The complexities of providing a program of required courses in a large, multi-curricula university have not permitted much of the sort of planning implied by the previous paragraphs. Students do not, indeed cannot, take the Basic courses at the same time or in the same sequence. We have been forced to think more in terms of courses and less in terms of a program. The result is that these studies barely touch on this problem of organization of learning experiences. One reference in Chapter 15 to experimentation with the use of a nondirective, student-centered technique of instruction does suggest that such an approach must be introduced cautiously and gradually lest certain types of students be antagonized to the point where the possible values of the approach are negated. Interpreting educational experiences in a more extended sense—inclusive of counseling, remedial services, provisions for acceleration, and policies in regard to choice and change of major—the follow-through study by Warrington discussed in Chapter 4 will ultimately yield evidence as to how these various educational experiences are related in the progress and ultimate graduation of our students.

Ideally, the results of testing and evaluation should be helpful in determining the relative difficulty of concepts and ideas. Likewise, evaluation studies could be helpful in assessing the difficulty of various types of material and appropriate placement of them in the curriculum. At Michigan State, as the Basic courses have been repeatedly revised, judgments based on previous experience have been the primary basis for decisions involving continuity and sequence. Interdepartmental discussion groups have helped to acquaint the faculty generally with all the courses and to develop some informal relations between them in addition to the pervasive theme of the nature of man and his works.

And Necessary

The fourth stage in curriculum planning is evaluation. Some possible contributions of evaluation to the selection of objectives and to the planning and organization of learning experiences have been suggested. Evaluation should have contributed to curriculum planning in the studies of students and of contemporary society. The initial selection and organization of experiences are based primarily on staff judgment. A curriculum or even a single course is such a complex pattern of experiences, however, and the students, teachers, and objectives introduce so many variables, that there can be no assurance that the program developed will produce the results desired. Only through a continuing program of evaluation can the strengths and weaknesses be identified so that replanning and improvement can be a continuing process.

The judgments of experienced teachers in close contact with students make up a common and certainly an important type of evaluation. Presumably, these judgments will be more valid if they are based upon formal evaluation activity such as studies of student progress or studies utilizing the relative progress of groups of students exposed to different materials, methods, and activities. However, few generalizations can be made about learning experiences that are valid for all teachers, all students, and all objectives. This suggests that each school and each teacher must engage in such evaluation and interpret the results in relation to the local or personal situation. This is fortunate, for the insights and questions which are a part of the evaluation process are frequently as important as the results in suggesting possible ways to improve the curriculum. With every change—be it in the students, the teachers, or the curriculum—comes the necessity for further evaluation. The process never ends.

Part II

ABOUT
OUR STUDENTS

3

EDWARD A. CARLIN

Of Those Who Begin

To an outsider, the members of a strange tribe are likely to appear remarkably homogeneous. At first glance, so does a new freshman class. But sensitivity to the differing interests and aspirations and the wide range of talent, training, and ability among incoming freshmen may lead to the opposite conclusion that no two freshmen are alike. Further reflection, of course, suggests the more productive hypothesis that they are neither entirely alike nor are they completely different from each other.

Data gathered on the entering freshmen at Michigan State University in the Fall of 1954 bear this out. This group of 3,215 students were amazingly varied in many ways, but similarities and patterns do exist, particularly in their socio-economic backgrounds.

Their Origins

In the matter of geographic origins, for example, the students came from 65 foreign countries and from 47 of the 48 states; yet 78.7 per cent of the men and 85 per cent of the women came from Michigan and adjacent states. Table 1 includes other information on geographic origin. The typical Michigan State freshman is a midwesterner and most likely comes from Michigan itself.

31

TABLE 1

GEOGRAPHIC ORIGINS OF MSU FRESHMEN
FALL 1954

Description	Men		Women	
	No.	%	No.	%
Michigan	1212	66.5	956	71.7
Contiguous	223	12.2	177	13.3
N. Y., N. J., Pa.	172	9.4	64	4.8
Foreign	30	1.6	15	1.1
All Others	147	8.1	94	7.1
No Response	38	2.1	27	2.0
Total	1822	99.9	1333	100.0

Table 2 shows the per cent of freshman men and women who
came from various-sized communities. About 40 per cent of both
men and women come from cities of 25,000 population or over,
with 23 per cent of the men and 22 per cent of the women

TABLE 2

SIZE OF HOME COMMUNITY OF MSU FRESHMEN
FALL 1954

Description	Per Cent of Men	Per Cent of Women
Open Country	8.1	5.3
Under 1000	7.5	7.7
1000–2500	11.0	12.1
2500–10,000	16.7	16.7
10,000–25,000	14.7	16.5
25,000–100,000	17.8	18.4
Over 100,000	23.3	22.1
No Response	0.9	1.3

coming from population centers of 100,000 or more. This is not surprising, given the population distribution of the state, but it does show that the appeal of this land-grant institution is no longer limited to the rural areas.

Table 3 gives the per cent of freshman men and women in various sizes of high school graduating classes. The majority of the freshmen were in graduating classes numbering over 100. The

TABLE 3

SIZE OF HIGH SCHOOL GRADUATING CLASS OF MSU FRESHMEN
FALL 1954

Description	Per Cent of Men	Per Cent of Women
25 or Less	5.9	3.4
26–50	13.4	12.0
51–75	12.5	12.6
76–100	12.5	8.3
101–150	13.2	14.7
151–200	7.5	7.5
201–300	11.8	12.7
301–400	9.2	13.2
Over 400	10.2	14.6
No Response	2.5	0.9
Non-Graduate	1.4	0.1

data on home community and class size suggest that a significant portion of this entering class must already have been familiar with urban and bureaucratic organization. Even so, an institution of some 18,000 students may present some new problems. Almost 20 per cent of the freshman men and 15 per cent of the freshman women came from small high schools having 50 or less in the graduating class. For these students, entrance into a large institution where the urban way of life is the dominant background of many students must require some readjustment.

Their Ages

Chronological age and school grade are so correlated in American education that it is no surprise to find that over 93 per cent of the freshman women were 18 years of age or but slightly younger. Although only 65 per cent of the men were in this group, those who had served in the armed forces (over 22 per cent) accounted for most of the difference. Although the large majority of these freshman students were 17 to 18 years old, the range included some who had not yet reached their seventeenth birthday and others who had already passed their thirty-sixth.

Marital Status

A generation ago the married undergraduate student was a rarity. In 1954, 7 per cent of the entering freshman male students were married, and less than 2 per cent of entering freshman women were married. Other data available indicate that the percentage of women students who are married increases markedly from the freshman to the sophomore year. Housing developments on the campus pay tribute to the acceptance of the married undergraduate, and school offices gladly employ the nonstudent wives; questions regarding possible implications for the curriculum have yet to be raised.

Socio-Economic Backgrounds

In a study of a group of persons the majority of whom are under twenty years of age, it is a sound sociological approach to gather some data on their parents. These students, therefore, were asked to describe their fathers' occupations and to indicate the basis upon which he received his income. The information was coded according to the United States Census Classification. Students were also asked to provide information about the educational attainments of their fathers and mothers. The data on fathers' occupations are reproduced in Table 4.

TABLE 4

OCCUPATIONS OF THE FATHERS OF FRESHMEN ENTERING MSU
FALL 1954

Description	Per Cent for Men	Per Cent for Women
Professional	11.2	15.3
Farmer	8.9	7.7
Prop., Mgr., Off.	30.0	40.9
Clerk and Kindred	11.6	10.4
Skilled and Foreman	29.0	21.4
Semi-Skilled	4.3	1.7
Farm Laborer	0.2	0.1
Other	0.5	0.2
Servant Class	0.7	0.2
Deceased, Retired	3.3	1.8
No Response	0.4	0.5

OCCUPATIONS OF FATHERS

While these data do not contain staggering surprises, they do disclose interesting relationships. For example, in comparing the occupational levels of the fathers of men and the fathers of women students, it is apparent that the fathers of the women tend toward employment in the upper levels of the occupational scale. The inference is that a college education is still regarded as somewhat of a luxury for women. The percentage of students whose fathers' occupations are in the professional or the proprietor, managerial, and official classification is larger than the proportion of those classifications in either the state or the nation. Substantial percentages (29 per cent for men, 21.4 per cent for women) of the students' fathers are in the skilled and foreman classifications. Since these latter occupational classifications do not require higher educational attainment, one might guess that the sons and daughters of this group are socially mobile persons who regard college as a route to social and occupational advancement.

Another way of looking at these data is to note the large percentage of the fathers of these students who come from "white collar" occupations. The fathers of over 50 per cent of the men and of over 65 per cent of the women may be so classified. The fathers who are not white collar workers are mostly skilled workers or foremen. This generalization is given further support by Table 5 which shows the ways in which the fathers of these students receive their income. If we add the percentages who received income in the form of salary, profit, commission, and fee, the "white collar" totals are 67 per cent for the fathers of freshman men and 78 per cent for the fathers of freshman women.

In contrast, income in the form of wages or piece-rate (both more typically associated with unskilled or semi-skilled labor) is reported for only 29 per cent of the fathers of freshman men and 20 per cent of the fathers of freshman women. However, from a

TABLE 5

FORM OF INCOME RECEPTION OF FATHERS OF FRESHMEN
FALL 1954

Description	Per Cent for Men	Per Cent for Women
Piece Rate	2.5	1.4
Wage Rate	26.9	17.9
Salary Rate	37.0	45.2
Profit	21.4	22.8
Commission	4.9	4.3
Fee	3.3	5.6
Dividend or Interest	0.6	0.9
Other; Retired	1.4	0.9
No Response	1.9	1.1
Don't Know	0.1	—
Response Modified	1.3	1.6

different perspective one might be surprised that the children of wage- and piece-rate income receivers constitute even this large a percentage of the total student population. This situation could be construed as evidence that the open class characteristics of American society are retaining their vitality. Such a conclusion gains additional support from examination of the educational backgrounds of the fathers of these students.

PARENTAL EDUCATION

A comparison—see Table 6—of the educational attainments of the freshman fathers with the educational attainments of the male population of over 25 in the state of Michigan shows that the fathers of these freshmen have had more education than is characteristic of the male population of the state of Michigan. For example, according to the 1950 census of population, almost 43 per cent of all Michigan males had attained no more than an

TABLE 6

EDUCATION OF FATHERS OF FRESHMEN
COMPARED WITH EDUCATION OF MICHIGAN MALES

Description	Per Cent for Men	Per Cent for Women	Per Cent of All Michigan Males *
Less than Grammar School	6.0	2.3	20.9
Completed Grammar School	18.4	14.1	21.9
Some High School	17.2	13.3	20.6
Completed High School	26.5	26.7	21.9
Some College	12.6	16.8	6.9
Completed College	10.4	14.7 ⎱	5.3
Prof. or Graduate School	7.3	11.4 ⎰	
No Response	1.6	0.8	2.6

* *1950 Census of Population. Vol. II, Part 22, p. 54, Table 20.*

elementary school education. This level of educational attainment accounted for a little more than 24 per cent of the fathers of freshman men and a little more than 16 per cent of fathers of freshman women. On the other hand, more than 17 per cent of the fathers of freshman men and 26 per cent of the fathers of freshman women had completed at least four years of college—contrasted with a little more than 5 per cent for the male population of the state.

A comparison of the educational attainments of the fathers of freshman men with those of the fathers of freshman women discloses a higher attainment for the latter group. About 30 per cent of the fathers of freshman men have had some college education while 41 per cent of the fathers of freshman women have had one or more years of college education.

The data on fathers' education indicate that the fathers of the freshman class of 1954 attained a higher educational level than the male population of over 25 for the state of Michigan as a whole. However, the majority of the fathers of both the male and female students had had no college education.

Data were also obtained on the educational attainments of the students' mothers. Only at the level of professional or graduate school attendance did the percentage of fathers exceed the percentage of mothers.

In order to look at the educational attainments of the parents of these students in a different way, the data on the educational attainments of both parents were examined jointly. Although the percentage of cases where both parents have completed college is not large, the percentage of cases where one or the other parent has had some college education is sizeable. Only 8.3 per cent of men and 9.9 per cent of women reported that both parents had completed four years of college. But 42.1 per cent of the men and 53.6 per cent of the women reported that at least one parent had had some education beyond high school. On the other hand, approximately 10 per cent of the men and 5 per cent of the women reported that their parents did not attend high school. In the remainder of the cases one or both parents at least attended high school with approximately 14 per cent of both men and women stating that their parents had completed high school and terminated their education at that point.

These data support the belief that parents seek greater educational attainments for their children than they have themselves enjoyed. There is also strong support for the proposition that this movement toward increased educational attainments from one generation to the next is an orderly one. While proof for this proposition lies beyond these data, they do seem to suggest that parents who have themselves attended high school or college expect their offspring to attend college. Those parents who have themselves attained something less than a high school education are not nearly as likely to send their offspring to college. There is evident also a sex differential—in families of lower social or educational status, daughters are less likely to attend college than are the sons. Perhaps higher education is regarded more as a necessity for men and as a luxury for women.

READING OPPORTUNITIES AND HABITS

The students were asked to list all of the magazines that could be regularly found in their homes. Only 5 per cent of the men and 2 per cent of the women reported that no magazines were regularly found in their homes. In over 75 per cent of the homes of both men and women it was reported that three or more magazines could regularly be found. When these magazines were classified according to type it was discovered that most frequently the pictorials—*Life, Look,* and similar magazines—were to be found. The pictorials were followed by the feature fiction like *The Saturday Evening Post, Colliers,* etc., and the pocket and digest type of magazine such as *The Reader's Digest* and *Coronet.* Literary periodicals such as *The Atlantic Monthly* and *Harper's Magazine* were found in less than 3 per cent of the homes of freshman men and in about 4 per cent of the homes of freshman women. News weeklies, like *Time* and *Newsweek,* were to be found in about one-third of the homes, but only one student in five reported that he read these magazines regularly.

It is safe to say that the literary fare available in the homes of most of these students is not challenging. Digests, slick fiction, and pictorials have carried the day.

The previous activities of our students did not include a burning interest in current affairs if interests can be measured by the time spent in reading newspapers, news magazines, or listening to radio or television newscasts. About half of the men and less than half of the women reported that they read a newspaper every day. About the same percentages of both men and women reported that they listened to a radio newscast every day. No more than a fifth of the men or women reported that they regularly read a weekly news magazine. In fact, the most frequently recorded response relative to the reading of news magazines was that they read them "now and then."

Activities and Organizations

A number of questions were asked of these students relative to their activities previous to attendance at Michigan State University. The answers demonstrated clearly that these young people had been busy. There might be some disposition to quarrel with the nature of some of their efforts, but they were active. The students were asked to list all of the organizations to which they had belonged while attending high school. Table 7 shows the results. Only 4 per cent of the women students reported that they did not belong to an organization of any kind during their high school careers, while 21 per cent of the men reported no organizational membership. Not only did the women students report that they belonged to more organizations than did the men students, but larger percentages of them belonged to almost every type of high school organization. The largest single group of both men and women belonged to those organizations designated as "service," a category including student government, student union, assembly committee, fire guards, etc. The fact that almost seven of every ten women reported membership in such groups in contrast to the two out of five men suggests two not necessarily mutually exclusive possibilities. It may be that the women students are more likely to identify with organizations designed to render service to some larger group. It may be, on the other hand, that this is one more indication of the somewhat higher social status of the women students and the selective factors involved in their college attendance. That is, it may be that the higher status individuals belong to those organizations that can be identified as being closely allied with the school administration.

TABLE 7

PARTICIPATION OF FALL 1954 FRESHMEN IN
HIGH SCHOOL STUDENT ORGANIZATIONS AND ACTIVITIES

Description	Per Cent for Men	Per Cent of Women
Athletic	30.8	32.9
Music	17.9	40.4
Service	43.4	67.5
Interest and Hobby	31.5	59.6
Scholarship	5.7	14.0
Fraternal	13.7	24.2
Religious	2.7	6.0
Vocational	9.2	17.9
Other	6.1	9.1
None	21.1	4.0

Work Experience

That the activities of these students were by no means restricted to membership in high school organizations is indicated by Table 8, which summarizes the responses to a series of questions relative to the amount and kind of paid jobs held before coming to Michigan State. Only 2.3 per cent of the men reported no work for pay, and only 10 per cent of the women made this same response. As Table 8 shows, many of these students had held a full-time job for a period. As might be expected, the jobs held were in areas that required little training or experience. The largest single group of men, for example, reported that they held jobs which could be classified as unskilled manual labor while the largest single group of women reported jobs that would be classified as clerk and waitress. The types of jobs held probably reflect the areas in which temporary employment is most easily found. While it is safe to say that the vast majority of these students have worked at jobs comparable to those held by the working class, it would be an error to impute to them on that account the sharing or even understanding of working class attitudes or values. It is quite likely that these students viewed their employment as temporary and separate from their other life experiences.

TABLE 8

PAID JOBS HELD BY MSU FRESHMEN
PRIOR TO COLLEGE ATTENDANCE

Description	Per Cent of Men	Per Cent for Women
No Job	2.3	10.1
Part Time During School	45.1	53.2
Full Time During School	4.3	1.4
Part Time During Summer	15.1	24.2
Full Time During Summer	58.1	55.1
Part Time No School	1.6	1.1
Full Time No School	16.3	7.5
Military Service	21.7	0.2
Other	3.0	2.1
No Response	1.9	1.8

Academic Achievement and Educational Plans

While engaging in many extra-curricular activities in high

school and demonstrating at the same time that they have no aversion to work for pay, these students were able to attain respectable academic standings as compared with their fellow high school students. Between 40 and 50 per cent of the men were in the upper third of their high school graduating class and between 66 and 73 per cent of the women were also in the upper third of their graduating class.

The members of this freshman class were asked a series of questions about the amount and kind of higher education they expected to obtain. An analysis of the student responses to these questions indicates a dominant interest in curricula that will provide vocational training. Over 26 per cent of the men want a program that will lead to a career in engineering, and around 20 per cent want training for some phase of business. The responses of the women students also followed a vocational pattern. For women, however, training for teaching constituted the largest single percentage of responses.

The tendency in American society to expect that formal education will supply specific vocational training helps one to understand the curricula choices that these students have made. The existence of these strong vocational aims, however, can be the source of misunderstanding and tension, because the university requires educational experiences in addition to those designed for the direct satisfaction of the students' vocational aspirations. The probability that the purposes of a general, nonvocational educational program may be only dimly perceived by these students implies a need for considerable interpretation of the program if it is to be successful. However, as data reported in Chapter 6 indicate, our students ultimately value—if they do not do so immediately—the general education aspects of a college education.

The vast majority of these students want to complete at least four years of college education. In fact, less than 2 per cent of the men indicated that they desired anything under four years. However, a little more than 10 per cent of the women students indicated that two years of college was all they really wanted.

An interesting piece of information concerning the amount of education these students would like to have is the fact that 30 per cent of the men indicated that they hoped to attend graduate school and about 15 per cent stated that they definitely planned to attend graduate school. Since these responses were made at the very beginning of these students' careers in college, they seem remarkable. While the number of women who expect to attend graduate school is smaller, the 12 per cent who indicated such a desire again seems surprisingly large.

It may be that the educational aspirations of these freshman students are totally unrealistic. However, the percentages who may actually apply for graduate school could be much smaller than these figures predict and still be a source of numerous problems. In any case, the very fact that such a considerable number of freshmen aspire to more than four years of college education suggests that just as the college degree has, in many areas, replaced the high school diploma as the minimum acceptable level of educational attainment, so in the future the goal of a Bachelor's degree may be replaced by completion of at least a year or two of graduate training.

Does such a development mean that the undergraduate programs should become increasingly general and unspecialized? Does it imply some differentiation at the undergraduate level as larger numbers seek to prepare themselves for graduate study? Does it mean that differentiation at the graduate level must be made in terms of terminal, professional, and technical degree work as distinct from the traditional graduate programs? Does it mean that the university must develop more reliable instruments for the selection of those who can profit by graduate study? If wholesale waste and frustration are to be avoided, many other questions must be raised and answered, but these give some indication of the problems that may face the university if more and more students aspire to and expect graduate study.

Table 9 provides information about when students reached the decision to attend college. Almost 63 per cent of the women reported that their plans to attend college dated as far back as they could remember, and about 41 per cent of the men made the same response. Less than 4 per cent admitted to reaching the decision within the month before college opened. Apparently the decision to attend college was for the majority of these students one of long standing, not dependent upon any particular event or accident. As a matter of fact, very few students felt that any particular event or person influenced their decisions to attend college. Less than 2 per cent reported that a scholarship constituted the critical factor in college attendance for them. This pattern raises some doubt as to the success of a scholarship program in encouraging able high school graduates to attend college if, in their earlier years, they have not planned in that direction. Early identification, continued motivation, and some assurance of the possibility of college attendance may be required.

TABLE 9

TIME WHEN PLANS WERE MADE TO ATTEND COLLEGE

Description	Per Cent of Men	Per Cent of Women
Long as Can Remember	41.1	62.9
During High School	32.6	27.9
Within Last Month	3.7	3.9
During Military Service	16.9	0.2
Other	5.4	5.0
No Response	0.2	0.1

Summary

Factual data and statistics such as those presented in this chapter are not immediately and obviously helpful to the teacher in the classroom. But they do provide some insight into the backgrounds of students. Occasionally they may even drive home the point to a faculty member that students at a midwest state university are not altogether like those in more selective institutions. In this connection it would be helpful if comparable data were available on a state and national level by type of institution.

Perhaps the greatest value of such compilations would be found by repeating them from time to time in some institution in order to determine whether there are systematic changes in the type of students admitted. If there are such changes, it is desirable to know their nature on some quantifiable basis. As enrollment increases, we hope to repeat this survey one or more times with just such purposes in view.

4

WILLARD G. WARRINGTON

Some Remain

The Longitudinal vs. the Cross-Sectional Approach

To varying degrees on all college campuses there is information available concerning the status of the students enrolled for a given quarter or semester as to academic performance, curriculum choice, extra-curricular activities, withdrawal actions, and many other variables associated with a college career. Usually, these data are classified by class, sex, major, and other pertinent variables so as to yield information valuable or necessary from the administrative and planning point of view. However, this type of cross-sectional report does not provide any indication of progress or change over a period of time for a particular group of students. Questions such as "What per cent of an entering group successfully graduate?" or "How stable are initial curricular choices?" can never be answered by cross-sectional data alone.

Snapshots preserve a pose or an instant of activity, but a series of snapshots or movies provides a dynamic record of the activity. Thus we might say that longitudinal data—that is, data compiled systematically for the *same* subject over some time span—are the movies of educational research. Such data may be obtained by two approaches. One is the historical approach, in which a group of subjects are identified—for instance the graduating class of 1955—and data pertaining to earlier experience are obtained from available records. This is usually the most expedient method of collecting longitudinal data if extensive records are carefully kept. But when research is an afterthought it is commonly found that the records are far from complete and that nothing can be done to complete them. Furthermore, such retrospective research does not usually reveal much about those who failed to reach the stage from which the study begins.

The second type of longitudinal study actually follows the subjects through an experience as it happens. Here the disadvantage lies in the time span involved. If one wishes to study college careers he must plan the study to cover four or more years and curb his impatience, and that of others, at the delay. The advantages may outweigh this disadvantage. More complete records can be kept and, as new variables become significant, the researcher may even be able to adjust his data-collecting procedures accordingly. Probably even more important, since the researcher is involved in the events, the analysis of this type of data is likely to be more perceptive and valuable. This possibility is further enhanced by partial analyses as segments of the data become available.

The Follow-Through Study of the Students Entering Michigan State in the Fall of 1953

This chapter is primarily a partial analysis of incomplete data on the most elaborate longitudinal study which we have yet undertaken—a follow-through study of the 4,223 students who entered Michigan State for the first time in the fall of 1953. Data are being accumulated for each individual for each term completed in these basic variables: grades for the term and cumulative grade point average, credits carried and earned, courses accelerated, courses repeated, stability of curriculum choice, use of Counseling Center, registration and performance in Improvement Services, time of dropout, and status at time of dropout. Considerable background data are available for each student, thereby permitting comparison of various subgroups within the larger study population. Examples of background data are: reading, arithmetic, English, and critical thinking abilities as measured by the orientation test battery; size and type of high school attended, or for transfer students, the type of institution transferred from; military status; marital status; and the usual characteristics such as sex, age, citizenship, and home address.

PURPOSES OF THE STUDY

The data collected can be classified into three broad categories. *First,* data are being collected that will help us design better sampling procedures for selecting representative subgroups within our student populations. For example, prior to this study we had no complete information available as to the location and type of institutions that our transfers were coming from nor the number and kinds of credits that they were transferring. We now have information that would be most helpful in selecting a representative sample of, say, transfer students from junior colleges who are presently enrolled at Michigan State.

Second, the data concerning the progress of a large number of students will enable us to study the longitudinal effects of many variables on student behavior over the total time spent in college. Consider, for example, the question "Does the student who earns college credit by examination under our acceleration program graduate early, earn additional credits, or simply take lighter loads than the nonaccelerating students?" This can best be answered by continued scrutiny of the accelerating students' academic records.

Third, since data are recorded for each student we will be able to study the interrelationships of many aspects of the college program, rather than the isolated effect of each variable separately. To illustrate, Michigan State has a liberal attitude toward permitting students to change their choice of major preference. We hope to discover concomitant effects of such changes on other variables related to success or failure in the college situation.

DESIGNATION OF SUBGROUPS

The 4,223 students who entered Michigan State for the first

time in the Fall of 1953 were subdivided into seven basic subgroups on three variables:

1. *Sex.* Since available evidence indicates differences in performance and treatment of males and females in the college situation it seemed necessary to consider the two sexes separately.

2. *Prior attendance at another college.* Students transferring from another academic institution are often treated little differently than freshmen. Hence, transfer students are not well understood even though their numbers are continually growing. We need to know more about them to determine whether special provisions are needed to ease their transition from one college to another.

3. *Attendance at summer counseling clinic.* Michigan State for several years has conducted a series of three-day summer counseling clinics for new students. The students take several tests, meet with counselors, and are generally oriented to the program and campus of Michigan State. This is a voluntary program which involves some financial outlay on the part of the student. Considerable interest in the effects of these clinics has developed. The inclusion of this variable should provide some relevant information.

Table 10 shows the numbers in the seven basic subgroups used throughout the study. The group of "specials" is a miscellany of part-time students, nondegree students, foreign students with unevaluated work from foreign institutions, and other students with unusual programs. Data for this special group have limited value beyond accounting for *all* new students entering in the fall of 1953.

Two observations are pointed up by Table 10:

1. Over one in five of our new students are actually not new to higher education at all but have attended other academic institutions.

2. More than a third of our new freshmen make their first formal contact with Michigan State during their attendance at a summer counseling clinic.

TABLE 10

BASIC SUBGROUPS FOR STUDY OF THE
NEW STUDENTS ENTERING FALL 1953

Subgroup Description	Number		% of Total Group	
Transfers				
1. Males	558		13.2	
2. Females	291		6.9	
Total transfers		849		20.1
Freshmen				
3. Males, attended counseling clinic	559		13.2	
4. Males, did not attend counseling clinic	1295		30.7	
Total males		1854		43.9
5. Females, attended counseling clinic	591		14.0	
6. Females, did not attend counseling clinic	804		19.0	
Total females		1395		33.0
Total freshmen		3249		76.9
7. Specials	125	125	3.0	3.0
Total group		4223		100.

"Transfer" students and "counseling clinic" students constitute sufficiently large groups to have considerable significance for planning our program.

WHAT ARE OUR ENTERING STUDENTS LIKE?

As expected, our new students include more males than females (59% to 41%). However, within the subgroups there are some interesting variations in the sex ratio. For example, there are proportionately more male transfers than females (66% to 34%).

One might speculate that male students being more vocationally oriented are more likely to transfer from one institution to another to obtain specific vocational preparation.

Only 30 per cent of the freshman males attended the summer clinics whereas 42 per cent of the freshman females participated, making a sex ratio in the summer program slightly in favor of the females. It may be that more male students are employed during the summer, or it may be that females have more worries about college and wish to take advantage of all resources that might help to insure success. A combination of several such factors may be involved.

Transfer students are a somewhat older and more heterogeneous group than freshmen. Those freshmen attending summer counseling clinics are slightly younger and somewhat more homogeneous agewise than those freshmen not attending a clinic. Relatively few of the freshman veterans (27 of 241) have chosen to attend the clinics. Omitting these veterans, the entering freshmen fall largely in the age group 17 to 19.

ORIGINS OF THE STUDENTS

Approximately 79 per cent of these entering students came from Michigan and another 9 per cent from the three states (Illinois, Indiana, and Ohio) immediately adjacent to the south. Another 4 per cent came from New York, 6 per cent from the remaining states, and 2 per cent from foreign countries. There is remarkable similarity in the pattern of geographic distribution for the various subgroups, with the exception of the special group which had a disproportionate number of foreign students. Students attending summer counseling clinics came from virtually the same general areas as those students not attending these clinics.

Only two Michigan counties were not represented in the entering students of fall 1953. However, nearly 50 per cent of the in-state entering students came from four counties: the local county of Ingham; Kent County, which includes Grand Rapids;

and Wayne and Oakland, which include most of greater Detroit. This percentage, based on in-state students, is about the same for freshmen (45.7%) and transfers (50.1%). More than one of three (37.4%) of *all* entering students are from the above mentioned four counties.

The 849 transfer students transferred credits from more than 222 different academic institutions located in 36 states and many foreign countries. The largest proportion (534) of this group transferred from 43 different academic institutions located within Michigan.

Over a third (37.5%) of the total entering transfer group came from junior colleges. All 13 of the Michigan junior colleges were represented, with the largest contingents (48 students each) coming from the Flint and Grand Rapids Junior Colleges. The 257 students transferring from degree-granting institutions within Michigan came from 26 different institutions.

The 3,249 freshmen came from 1,064 high schools located in 37 different states. The largest proportion, 2,541 (78.2%), came from 497 high schools located in Michigan. Some high schools sent large contingents—120 from Lansing Sexton and 79 from Lansing Eastern—but 307, or 62 per cent, of the Michigan high schools sent 3 or less students and 142, or 29 per cent, sent only 1 student.

DIFFERENCES IN ABILITIES

As a part of the orientation program, all new students are given an English Usage test, an Arithmetic test, a Reading test, and the American Council on Education Psychological Examination. Transfer students score considerably higher on the orientation tests than do the freshmen. To determine whether the transfer group was originally more capable or whether the education already received has increased their mean scores, we plan to compare the transfers with the freshmen after they have completed an equivalent amount of work.

These data clearly support the difference favoring females in

TABLE 11

ATTRITION IN THE FOLLOW-THROUGH GROUP

Subgroups	No. Entering Fall 1953	Per Cent Returning Winter 1954	Per Cent Returning Spring 1954	No. and Per Cent Returning Fall 1954		Per Cent Returning Winter 1955	Per Cent Returning Spring 1955	No. and Per Cent Returning Fall 1955	
				N	%			N	%
Transfers									
Males	558	91	89	426	76	73	72	285	51
Females	291	91	88	199	68	64	61	94	32
Total	849	91	89	625	74	70	68	379	45
Freshmen									
Males, counseling clinic	559	95	93	470	84	80	78	402	72
Males, no counseling clinic	1295	91	85	916	71	67	65	786	61
Females, counseling clinic	591	97	93	474	80	77	75	386	65
Females, no counseling clinic	804	94	89	546	68	64	62	406	50
Total	3249	93	89	2406	74	70	68	1980	61

verbal abilities and males in quantitative ability. However, the sexes seem about equal on the total psychological score. Students who attend the summer clinics are slightly superior to those who do not. Further analysis of the orientation test data for the transfer group indicates that students from four-year institutions generally score higher than those transferring from junior colleges. We do not yet know whether these differences are reflected in subsequent performance of these students at Michigan State.

The Follow-Through Group After Two Years

HOW MANY ARE GONE?

Attrition, used here to mean leaving college before the attainment of an educational goal, is a major concern to many persons in higher education. The data presented in Table 11 summarize the attrition in the follow-through group by terms over the first two years of the study.

An analysis of these data suggests several interesting observations:

1. Attrition in the study group was generally greater during the first year than during the second: 26 per cent of the freshmen dropped out by the end of their first year whereas only 13 per cent dropped out during or at the end of their second year.
2. Attrition during the first two years is remarkably similar for the freshman and transfer groups. However, a considerably higher per cent of the freshmen return for their third year because many transfers earn degrees by the end of their second year.
3. The greatest attrition occurs between the spring and fall terms. This probably results from many factors. The end of an academic year is a natural stopping place for those not strongly motivated for a degree; little face is lost by the unsuccessful student who just doesn't return for the succeeding year; students taking jobs over the summer may find opportunities

and challenges more attractive than returning to college; more students are dropped at the end of spring term than at other times; and June weddings continue to be popular.

4. Attrition is greater for females than males. As discussed more in detail by Dr. Banzet in Chapter 5, students drop out of college for many reasons but, particularly for females, marriage is a common one which more than accounts for the difference.

5. Surprising was the smaller rate of attrition among those freshmen who attend a summer counseling clinic than among those freshmen who did not. This became apparent (for both females and males) beginning with the very first term after entrance. Whether this results entirely from the clinic participation is doubtful. Certainly we suspect that the motivation involved in clinic attendance would favor continuing in college. Data presented in the following pages will support this inference by demonstrating that the summer clinic students take advantage of other opportunities that are designed to increase the probability of a successful college career.

Although the proportion of transfer students returning for the third year is lower than for freshmen, the percentage of dropouts who attain no apparent educational goal is greater for freshmen. As indicated in Chapter 5, many students classified as dropouts actually transfer to other colleges. Plans are presently being made to attempt to obtain more information concerning the present status of these dropout students.

ACADEMIC PROGRESS

The gross summary of average academic status indicates that students remaining in college make academic progress about as expected. The average credits earned by freshmen at the end of their first year is somewhat above the 42 required for sophomore standing and at the end of their second year is again above the 92 required for junior status. Likewise, the grade point averages

(GPA) of the various subgroups are all above the required minimum C or 2.00 average. As usual, the GPA of females is above that of males. Transfers earn higher grades than the freshmen, and counseling clinic freshmen make higher marks than those who did not attend a clinic.

For each subgroup the mean grade point average is higher at the end of the second year than at the end of the first. To consider the effect of the selectivity involved in the dropping out of poorer students, we obtained the first year GPA for only those students who *completed* the second year and found that of this group the transfer students made somewhat lower grades during their first year (2.22—1st year, 2.57—2nd year) but that the freshmen performed at essentially the same level (2.47—1st year, 2.44—2nd year). This increase in GPA of the continuing transfer students seems to be related to the fact that by the second year most of these students are in an upper college where grades run higher. From previous experience, we predict that this same trend will manifest itself in the freshman group during the third and fourth years of the study.

Great variations exist within the various subgroups at the end of the two-year period. For example, the credits earned by freshmen enrolled for *all* six quarters during their first two years ranged from 138 to 43. Or, looking at these variations in another way, 171, or 7.8 per cent, of those freshmen completing their sixth quarter had gained more than a quarter's work over the average of their group and another 132, or 6 per cent, had fallen behind their group by more than a quarter's work. Students do not progress in the lock step that our administrative structure would suggest.

There are also great variations in the grade point averages that are not revealed in the group averages. GPA's for freshmen enrolled for all six quarters ranged from 3.96 (straight A is 4.00) to 1.19. Further evidence of the variability of academic performance is presented in Table 12.

TABLE 12

ACADEMIC HONORS AND DEFICIENCIES AT END OF TWO YEARS

Subgroup	*No. Completing Spring 1955*	*No. and Per Cent With GPA Above 3.50*		*No. and Per Cent With GPA Below 2.00*	
		N	*%*	*N*	*%*
Transfers					
Males	398	18	4.5	52	13.1
Females	175	7	4.0	8	4.6
Freshmen					
Males, counseling clinic	437	19	4.3	102	23.4
Males, no counseling clinic	825	22	2.7	212	25.7
Females, counseling clinic	441	21	4.8	68	15.4
Females, no counseling clinic	497	29	5.8	85	17.1

About one student in twenty has a cumulative grade point average of 3.50 (B+) or higher after two years. About one in five freshmen and one in ten transfers do not even have the 2.00 (C) average required for transfer to an upper college. These students must be dropped when they achieve junior status, although under some circumstances they are allowed to continue temporarily under Final Warning Probation. (Some data pertaining to the Final Warning program are discussed in Chapter 6.)

Approximately half (52% of transfers, 58% of freshmen) of the students who leave during or at the end of the first two years without receiving a degree or special terminal certificate have unsatisfactory records at the time of their withdrawal. The attitude toward this percentage will vary with the individual, but in any case the facts should be known to faculty and students alike.

TABLE 13

CURRICULUM CHOICES DURING FIRST TWO YEARS

Curriculum	Transfers						Freshmen					
	Males			Females			Males			Females		
	Fall 1953 %	Fall 1954 %	Fall 1955 %	Fall 1953 %	Fall 1954 %	Fall 1955 %	Fall 1953 %	Fall 1954 %	Fall 1955 %	Fall 1953 %	Fall 1954 %	Fall 1955 %
Agriculture	13.0	14.1	15.1	0.7	1.0	2.1	11.6	10.7	13.3	0.6	0.5	0.5
Business & Public Service	34.4	32.8	34.9	19.2	14.5	14.6	23.5	26.8	34.5	18.2	17.1	18.3
Engineering	19.5	19.2	17.8	0	0	0	23.9	22.0	19.6	0.1	0.2	0.1
Home Economics	0	0	0	15.5	16.1	19.8	0.1	0.1	0	15.1	16.2	17.6
Science and Arts	20.1	23.1	21.6	25.3	28.6	22.9	11.2	13.2	18.3	21.0	22.2	32.5
Veterinary Medicine	4.8	4.2	6.1	2.4	2.5	3.1	5.1	4.0	2.6	3.3	3.1	4.3
Education	1.9	2.3	2.0	32.6	34.7	34.4	2.0	2.1	4.4	15.1	19.4	24.1
No Preference	5.8	4.0	2.7	4.8	2.5	2.0	22.6	21.1	7.3	26.5	21.4	2.5

CURRICULUM CHOICE

Many students enroll at Michigan State without having reached decisions as to ultimate career or college major. Such students usually enroll as "no preference" students and utilize introductory courses and the services of the Counseling Center in making a specific preference choice. This choice must be made prior to the junior year but most students decide after three or four quarters. Changes from one curriculum choice to another are readily made upon approval by a counselor. To examine the effects of this program, we will consider the curriculum choices of the follow-through group initially at entrance, at the beginning of their sophomore year, and at the beginning of their junior year. To make Table 13 manageable, only preference choices by colleges are given.

The usual differences in preference choices between males and females are apparent from these data. The distribution of preference choices for the transfers remains fairly constant over the two-year period, but considerable variation is evident among the freshman distributions. This is primarily due to movement out of the "no preference" category. The proportion of freshman males choosing Engineering and Veterinary Medicine steadily decreases whereas most other choices hold constant or increase. Not many males initially in the "no preference" category later choose Engineering, and some students in Engineering drop out or change to other curricula. Majors in the Business and Public Service area, popular with freshman males at entrance, become even more popular two years later. For freshman women, Science and Arts and Elementary Education show the greatest gains in popularity over the two-year span.

In the face of the teacher shortage, it is encouraging to note that while only 7 per cent of the entering freshman males desired a teaching certificate, this percentage rose to 14 per cent two years later. The same figures for freshman females were 32 per cent at entrance and 53 per cent at the end of two years.

Data on preference changes indicate that nearly 40 per cent of our freshmen and 25 per cent of our transfers make *at least* one preference change during the first two years of their college careers. In fact, over 100 students in the follow-through group made two or more changes beyond their initial choice in their first two years of college work.

ACCELERATION

As discussed in Chapter 10, the acceleration by examination privilege is an integral part of the Basic College program. Nearly 18 per cent of the freshmen in the follow-through group attempted to take advantage of this privilege by securing special permission to obtain credit by examination in one or more Basic courses during their first two years. About 10 per cent of the entering freshmen received some credit. Most students accelerated in a single course (Communication Skills being the most common) but a few succeeded in two, three, or even more. Four students accelerated in six courses, one in seven, and one in eight. A higher proportion of females accelerate than males, and summer counseling clinic students accelerate more than the freshman students not attending such clinics.

REPEATING OF COURSES DURING FIRST TWO YEARS

Courses are often repeated in an attempt to raise a D grade or remove an F grade. Data for the first two years indicate that approximately 40 per cent of the freshman males repeat *at least* one course and that about 20 per cent of the freshman girls also found it necessary to repeat one or more courses. Of the transfers, about 25 per cent (30% of males, 18% of females) take one or more courses for the second time. In a few cases, courses were taken three or more times. The repetitions increase each term after admission, reaching a peak in the fifth and sixth terms— near the end of the sophomore year when transfer to an upper school requires a grade point average of C or higher.

We view these data with ambivalence. Repetition of courses

smacks somewhat of inefficient use of staff and facilities. Yet we have some evidence that the only way for many "borderline" students to make acceptable (2.00 GPA) progress toward a degree is to repeat every D (and of course F) grade that they receive; it is usually easier to make a C grade in a repeat course than a B grade in a new course. The real question is whether "borderline" students should be encouraged or discouraged. The answer to this question will undoubtedly depend, in part, upon the kind of institution in which this question is being considered. At a state-supported institution the dominant view is likely to be that students, once admitted, should be given every reasonable opportunity to succeed. Consequently, repeating courses is encouraged when this is the main barrier to continuance in school. Despite evidence of the effectiveness of the practice, students and many of their advisers resist course repetition.

IMPROVEMENT SERVICES

Michigan State maintains an extensive Improvement Services program in the areas of Writing, Speaking, Reading, and Arithmetic to identify and correct deficiencies early in the students' college careers. The data from this study indicate that approximately one in five transfers and one in three freshmen register in one or more Improvement Services courses during their first two years at Michigan State. Registration in the Improvement Services courses decreases rapidly after the first two terms but a few students are still enrolling during their sixth term. Perhaps as a result of the effectiveness of the orientation and counseling received in the summer program, counseling clinic students make extensive use of the Improvement Services.

COUNSELING CENTER CONTACTS

Michigan State maintains a Counseling Center which is described in some detail in Chapter 12. In the follow-through study, the date, purpose, and frequency of all contacts that students in the study group make with the Counseling Center are recorded. Over 40 per cent of the freshmen and 25 per cent of the transfers made *at least* one call at the Center. These calls varied from a simple request for vocational information to consideration of serious personal problems. There were more contacts during the first and second terms, a general slackening off for the next two terms, and then an increase again over the last two terms. This suggests fairly frequent problems associated with initial adjustment at college, a more or less tranquil period, and then renewed difficulties probably associated with situations that had developed as a part of their college career.

Summary of the Follow-Through Study to Date

This chapter is an incomplete report, but a few remarks may be in order concerning our overall reactions to the project at this stage in its development.

ON THE NEGATIVE SIDE

This type of project is cumbersome and time-consuming when high standards of accuracy are maintained. The workload is increased by the fact that students who proceed in "atypical" fashion add to the complexity. Unfortunately, we are learning from this study that there are fewer students who progress as conventionally expected than we would have guessed. With discontinuous attendance, changing majors, and the like to account for, it sometimes seems that irregularity is the rule. Clearly our negative reactions result from the complications of the task.

ON THE POSITIVE SIDE

Genuine interest is being demonstrated in the results of our study from a variety of sources, both on campus and at other institutions. Excellent cooperation is being received in our efforts to compile the data. Several specific research projects, including at least one doctoral thesis, have used data originating from the study.

The study has pointed up certain problems on which further

evidence is needed and in some cases has shown that certain pre-conceived ideas are incorrect. Even the fact that our data are indicating that the "nonregular" student is quite common has tended to create a more tolerant attitude toward irregularity. Of course the maximum fruits of this project will become apparent only after it is complete. At this point we can only say that we are looking forward to its completion with enthusiasm.

5

ERNEST M. BANZET

Some Drop Out

Both With and Without Apparent Reason

Prominent in the mythology of American higher education is the story of the dean who in his welcoming speech to a group of freshman students advised each to look at those on either side of him because "four years hence only one of you will be present at the graduation exercises." Present-day student mortality rates are not so heavy. Our statistics show that about 50 per cent of entering students fall by the wayside or at least do not complete a degree in our own institution. By no means all of this academic homicide results from the grades fired at students by the faculty. Counting as justifiable homicides those students officially sent to another resting place (7% to 10%) and adding those who retire of their own volition forewarned by the wounds already received (12% to 15%), the total casualty rate resulting from unsatisfactory scholarship is about 22 per cent. Another 2 per cent satisfactorily complete the two-year terminal programs in which they initially enrolled. The remaining 26 per cent of the 50 per cent loss represents unexplained dropouts, most of whom were doing satisfactory or even excellent work at the time of their demise.

A study might well be made of the effect on individuals of an unsuccessful stay in a college or university. We too blithely assume that a tour of a college campus can do no one any harm. It is possible that for some individuals failure in a college may have permanent effects. On the other hand, we should not too readily assume that this is always the case. In some small communities even brief attendance at a college or university may make the man of distinction. However, a careful study of a group of academic casualties is difficult; the individuals simply do not respond well to the usual questionnaire. (And who can blame them?) Other types of contact are expensive.

Early in our consideration of dropouts we decided to restrict our major attention to those students who at the time of discontinuance were still in the good graces of the institution. Thus, we restricted our study to students whose grade point averages were 2.2 or higher (C:2.00) and who were not under any disciplinary shadow at the time they left. We decided further to restrict it to a group who had at least 12 and not more than 188 credits at the time of withdrawal. By the lower limitation we eliminated the many part-time students who take a course or two for a quarter or two, as well as those who drop out during the first quarter. (We have found that as high as 3 per cent of an entering group of freshmen withdraw without a single grade.) Those with a sufficiently large number of credits to put them within one quarter of completing their degree were also regarded as presenting a special group of problems.

The limitations which we have mentioned made it possible to approach these dropouts as individuals who had been doing satisfactory work in the college and whose absence actually was a matter of concern to the administration. Over the four-year period 1951–1955, a total of 2,630 students—1,056 males and 1,574 females—met the standards set for inclusion in the survey. The survey was carried on continuously over this period with a postal card questionnaire and an individually-typed form letter being sent to each student. The students were asked why they had withdrawn and whether they expected to return and complete their degrees. Each student was also encouraged to write a personal letter about himself and his plans, or to ask for further information about his possible return to the university. At the least he was urged to fill out and return the postal card which included the questions concerning the date when he withdrew, his class, his reasons for withdrawing, whether he expected to return to Michigan State or to enter some other college or university, or whether he did not expect to return to college at all. Most of these letters were sent within a period of three or four months after the person's withdrawal.

The limitations placed on the group contacted made us rather optimistic about the rate of return to be expected. We received slightly under 60 per cent return. The year, term of withdrawal, number of credits, or sex made no essential difference in this return rate. About one-third of the students responded by letter or appeared in person; the remaining two-thirds used only the postal card reply. Men by a slight margin—36 per cent against 31 per cent for women—tended to reply by letter or in person.

But They All Have Reasons

The reasons which the students gave for withdrawing from the University were the ones usually noted in such studies: attendance at other schools, lack of finances, military service, marriage, ill health of the individual or some member of his family, and work or job opportunities.

The tabulation and interpretation of reasons was complicated by the fact that some students gave more than one reason for their failure to return to the campus. A common example was that of the young man who, lacking funds, decided to enter military service and return later under governmental subsidy. A number of the women indicated that because of lack of funds they had decided to marry, thereby suggesting to some of us— especially the single men—the need for investigating the marital motivations of young women. Another common double explanation coming from young women was that they had married and were attending other schools where their husbands were enrolled. Again, illness in the family may lead a person to change to a college or university nearer home. Of the 1,524 students responding nearly one-fourth gave some such compound reason for leaving.

Among the entire group, transfer to another college accounts for 30 per cent of the withdrawals. Many of this group are individuals transferring to a professional school for which a certain amount of undergraduate training is needed but for which a degree is not required. Marriage runs a close second to transfer to another college, and is followed by financial problems, work, and health. Attendance at another school is a little more frequent as a reason for the withdrawal of men; financial problems are almost twice as frequent with men; and military service is almost entirely a masculine reason for leaving school.

On the other hand, only 4 per cent of the men gave marriage as a reason for leaving college, whereas 40 per cent of the women checked this factor as a reason. Poor health is indifferent to sex. More women than men listed a job as a reason for withdrawal. For the men, of course, withdrawal was likely to end in induction into military service.

These differences do make some sense in terms of other knowledge about students in higher education. It is surprising that the difference between the sexes is not greater on the matter of transferring to another school as a reason for leaving college, for it would be anticipated that many more men than women would go on to professional training. This may be a selective response bias, or it may be related to the increasing tendency to complete a bachelor's degree before entering certain professional programs. The fact that more men than women gave financial problems as a reason for leaving college whereas more women than men gave work as a reason for leaving seems at first to be a little contradictory. From some of the replies, both oral and written, one would seem to be justified in concluding that with many of the men the giving of a financial reason corresponded to an intent on their part to complete their college program at a later date— possibly after the completion of military service. For the men, withdrawing from college to take a job, on the other hand, might reflect loss of interest or discouragement with regard to college. An occasional young woman presented the compound reason of getting married and working to help send her husband through school. It appears that whereas some girls get married because they lack money, others do so to remedy a boy friend's lack of money!

Classifying withdrawals according to the credit range in hours, with the classifications used corresponding closely to the number of hours required for classification as a freshman, sophomore, junior, or senior, the pattern of variation in regard to class status was found to be a complex one involving an interaction with the sex of the student. Attending another school was a reason given increasingly by the men as their withdrawal time corresponded to larger and larger numbers of credits. For women, however, attending another school showed no change from one class to another, although this reason was actually given somewhat less frequently by seniors than by those below that level. For both men and women the financial problem accounted for a decreasing proportion of the dropouts as the students progressed further along in school.

As we have noted, military service as a reason for withdrawal was primarily a reason given by men and it showed only minor variation from one credit range to another. Only five girls gave this as a reason for their withdrawal. Marriage, on the other hand, is primarily a reason given by women. Only 5 per cent of the freshman men withdrew for this reason; during the sophomore and junior years the figure decreased to 3 per cent, and then increased to six per cent in the senior year. For women, the percentage in the freshman year was 34, increasing to 40, 44, and finally to 48 per cent in the senior year. Health as a reason for withdrawal seemed, as one would expect, to be unrelated to the number of credits the student had achieved. Withdrawal to take a job varied little for the men from one credit range to another. For the women, however, this reason increased from 7 per cent at the freshman level through 9 per cent for both the sophomore and junior years, to 12 per cent at the senior level. One factor, perhaps, is that completion of a degree is not the vocational necessity for women that it is for men, so that discontinuance short of a degree seems less serious.

All Are Not Lost!

In the letter of inquiry the students were asked to indicate whether they expected to return to Michigan State, to enter some other college, or not to return to college at all. Of the students who replied, only 65 per cent answered the question concerning their future college plans. Thus, in our summary of future intentions we are dealing with only about 38 per cent of those to whom the questionnaire was originally sent. However, 30 per cent of the replies had indicated enrollment in another college so that the question regarding their future college plans was irrelevant.

Fifty-seven per cent of the students replying to the question on future plans indicated their expectation of re-entering Michigan State. There was a marked sex difference in the reply to this question. Eighty per cent of the men indicated their intent to re-enter college whereas only 47 per cent of the women did so. The sex difference also interacted with the number of credits acquired. The per cent of men expecting to re-enter varied but little in accordance with the number of hours which they had completed. For the women, 33 per cent of those at the freshman level indicated an intention to return, whereas 75 per cent of them at the senior level so responded. We noted earlier that slightly less than 60 per cent of all students responded to the survey and it would be reasonable to expect that those who were planning to re-enter Michigan State would reply in greater numbers than would those not expecting to re-enter. Accordingly, it would be erroneous to apply the overall 57 per cent hope of re-entering Michigan State against the original dropout group contacted. As we shall see later, a more appropriate figure would be 30 to 35 per cent of the entire group.

With regard to the definite expectation to enter another school, the per cent was rather small. Only 6 per cent indicated such plans and variations according to number of credits and sex were of minor importance. Recalling that 30 per cent of all the students replying had already entered another school and adding those planning to enter another school at some later date accounts for 34 per cent of all responding students as actual or potential enrollees at another college or university.

Twelve per cent indicated that they would like to re-enter college, a response so phrased as to indicate doubts about the possibilities of doing so. Eight per cent of the men and 17 per cent of the women indicated this state of mind. This corresponds to other evidence suggesting quicker acceptance on the part of women of termination of their college degree programs. On this question of hopes there was some variation from class to class but no meaningful pattern. A related set of responses is found in the "will not re-enter college" category. Twenty-five per cent of the students responding to the question of future college plans indicated that they would not re-enter college. Forty per cent of the women gave this indication as against only 9 per cent of the men, re-emphasizing again the unwillingness of the man who is able to handle college work to terminate without acquiring a degree.

This "will not re-enter college" response showed a marked tendency to decrease with the increasing number of credits achieved. Half of the freshman women withdrawing indicated "no return," but this decreased to 42 per cent for the sophomores, 27 per cent for the juniors, and 7 per cent for the seniors. For the men, the pattern was less consistent in that the percentage started with 12 in the freshman year, decreased from 9 to 3 in the sophomore and junior years, and then increased once again to 12 per cent for the senior year. This might suggest that, in some cases at least, the withdrawal of a man at the level of the senior year involves a more serious event than withdrawal somewhat earlier in the college program. However, the numbers here are too small for such definite conclusions.

Putting into a single table the various responses as to educational status and future plans yields Table 14. The per cents given here have been adjusted to refer to the entire group of respondents rather than only to those answering the questions regarding future educational plans. Again it must be kept in mind that the figures do not necessarily hold for the complete group of satisfactorily performing withdrawals originally selected.

TABLE 14

SUMMARY OF PRESENT EDUCATIONAL STATUS
AND FUTURE PLANS

Status or Plan	*Per Cent*
Already entered another school	30
Hope to enter another school	4
Plan to re-enter MSU	32
Would like to re-enter MSU	18
Do not plan to return to school	16
	100

Nevertheless it is still of interest to speculate as to the implications of such data in reference to the student mortality rate. The approximately 50 per cent rate mentioned at the beginning of this chapter refers to the proportion of an entering class which had received degrees by the end of four or five years. However, students who have already entered another educational program may have met their goals with us as completely and definitely as those who continue to a degree at Michigan State. Certainly they are neither dead nor missing in action. Some of those who definitely plan to return or go to another school will continue.

Table 14 shows that 66 per cent of the individuals responding are either already in college elsewhere or have definite expectations of continuing their education. What the figure would be for those who did not reply we do not know, but it is a fair guess that it would be less. Neither do we know what portion of the 66 per cent will ultimately attain some definite educational objective. It is clear, however, that counting only those who complete a degree in four years gives an unduly grim picture of student mortality. Phrased in terms of student plans which may require transfer to other colleges and extending the period of time to include those who return, the per cent achieving their educational goals may be well beyond 50 per cent. Using various assumptions and the data at hand we have guessed that 60 per cent may be a more accurate indication of the per cent of entering students who achieve their educational goal. We shall take another look at this in the following chapter.

An Unexpected Bonus

One of the interesting and to some extent unexpected products of the survey was the expression of student attitudes toward the inquiry and toward the University. No student expressed an unfavorable attitude toward the inquiry, and many made favorable comments. Michigan State is, of course, a large institution; because of this many of the students expressed surprise that their absence from the campus had been noticed officially.

Part of their surprise resulted from the receipt of an individually typed and signed letter. (Not everyone is able to recognize the "personalized" product of a robot typewriter.) We had no doubt—judging from the amount of correspondence which was generated with some of the students, and from the number who took the trouble to come into the office and look up the person who had written to them—that the survey had a significant effect in increasing the number of returns among this group of students. It would be of interest to try to estimate just what the impact was in this regard, but the collection of data for comparison purposes was regarded as a formidable and perhaps impossible task.

We are now convinced that such a follow-up can be justified entirely on the basis of the public relations value. Not infrequently a student who withdraws from school has certain dissatisfactions which may not be his primary reasons for withdrawal but which nevertheless operate to color his point of view toward the institution. In many cases, a friendly follow-up obliterates such unpleasant memories, perhaps just because of the interest evidenced or possibly because the follow-up contact actually clarifies the situation to the satisfaction of the person. We found that the survey did bring to light numerous student criticisms with regard to the married housing situation, overcrowded conditions in the residence halls, social life, and the like, although seldom were such irritations the real reason why the student left college.

Statistical studies and surveys do not always create good will. It was to us, then, a happy event to find such a project greeted so favorably both by our former students and by university administrators.

Conclusion

This survey was undertaken to find the factors causing the withdrawal from the University of students in good academic standing. Our earnest search for knowledge was reinforced by the hope that with some understanding of the reasons involved, it might be possible to encourage such students to return and complete their degree. Forewarned by our knowledge, we might even be able to work out procedures which would assist such students to remain in school.

Of the 60 per cent responding, 30 per cent indicated that they were attending another school. Few of these could have been prevailed upon to remain at MSU, since most were in a professional program not available with us. With the 15 per cent withdrawing for financial reasons, and the 7 per cent withdrawing to take a job, it is possible that some might have been prevailed upon to remain in school, although few of these students used the University facilities for financial assistance and part-time work.

Most of the students leaving for military service indicated their intent to return to college. Although students leaving for reasons of marriage and of health often did not make their problems known in advance, we found little that could have been done to assist them to remain in school. We were unable to arrive at any workable recommendations for identifying and aiding these withdrawing students, thereby reducing their number.

Among the students not already enrolled in some other college, some 50 to 60 per cent definitely planned to return to school and complete their college education. Only about 25 per cent indicated no expectation of return. We made no attempt to estimate the success of the survey in encouraging students to re-enroll, although the survey contact did lead some students to this decision. If the follow-up contact of these withdrawing students were made by an individual known to the student, we suspect the procedure would be even more effective in stimulating re-entry.

The good will created by the survey would alone justify the effort. This was most clearly indicated when at the conclusion of the four years of the survey it was proposed to discontinue the follow-up activity; deans and other administrators of the University insisted that some procedure should be worked out to continue the program. We have the satisfaction not only of knowing something more about why students left the University but of having aroused sufficient interest in the problem to result in the establishment on a continuing basis of a follow-up of all such withdrawals from the University.

6

PAUL L. DRESSEL

And Some Graduate

Mortality and Survival

In this chapter we report on what we have learned about students in their progress toward a degree. This includes data on the per cent of students who progress in regular fashion, a side-glance at special measures to help some marginal students, and finally a summary of some of the things these graduates have to say about us after they have completed their work.

From some points of view, there has been too much attention to the problem of student mortality in higher education. The very phrase "student mortality" has a morbid and, as some use it, a sadistic sound. The alternative "attrition" is no better. Student mortality is also a troublesome term when one attempts to name its complement. The plausible opposite, "student immortality," is scarcely appropriate for it might refer equally to the occasional perennial student or to the football hero. In Chapter 5, Banzet noted that many of the students withdrawing were actually continuing their education elsewhere or had full intent of returning to Michigan State. Only a study of ten to twelve years' duration would reveal with accuracy the per cent of an entering class which actually completes a degree. Ultimately the study under way by Warrington, partially reported in Chapter 4, should give some concrete data on this discontinuous group of degree seekers. At the moment we can only be sure that they do reduce the so-called student mortality rates.

Largely ignored, also, is that group of students who enroll initially for one of a limited number of two-year terminal programs and leave after the completion of the certificate requirements. This group, approximately 2 per cent of an entering class, is still so new to us that in our routine statistics they end up among the withdrawals. There are others who plan on less than four years of college but do not so indicate. If a definitive study of student survival is to be made, it should be done in terms of the educational goals set by students for themselves and not in terms of the acquiring of a degree. College is not the unitary experience it once was.

The integrity of a four-year educational experience as embraced in the liberal arts ideal has been destroyed—at least in midwestern state universities—by our emphasis on credits and courses, and our inclusion of terminal and pre-professional curricula. A quarter system, as we have it at Michigan State, permits new students to enter—and they do—at any one of four different times during the year. Students pause to refresh themselves or their bank accounts without formal notice to that effect. They enroll in nondegree or pre-professional curricula; they transfer easily from one institution to another as convenience, costs, changing purposes, and love affairs suggest; and they may even substitute other goals for the traditional B.A. degree. It is not necessarily bad that the four-year loaf is ready-sliced and we may agree that "half a loaf is better than none," but surely something of significance is lost in this piecemeal education. Nevertheless, if we provide it, we ought to evaluate student progress by the number of slices they want rather than in reference to the entire loaf.

Having presented this view, we must admit the difficulties involved. Student purposes are not always clear and they are subject to change. To ascertain accurately the educational goal of all entering freshmen in a large institution is an impossibility. In the rest of this chapter, we shall talk about those who progress toward a degree, but we shall avoid any implication of failure, student or institutional, for those who do not achieve it.

An Early Study

In 1951 Mr. Joseph Sheedy, then assistant to the Dean of the Basic College, completed an academic survey of the first three Basic College classes. This survey included the classes starting in the fall quarters of the years 1944, 1945, and 1946. The summary of this survey which examined the status of each group four years later is given in Table 15.

TABLE 15

STATUS OF THREE ENTERING CLASSES AFTER FOUR YEARS

Status	Entered 1944 %	Entered 1945 %	Entered 1946 %
Graduated 4 Years Later	33	37	40.5
Still in School	13	12	16.5
Voluntary Withdrawal			
Average or Above	25	19	13
Below Average	16	16	15
Dropped Because of Grades	10	12	12
No Grades	3	4	3

In each case a sizeable group continued in school progressing toward a degree. Three major factors operated to keep a number of students in school beyond the four-year period. The first of these was discontinuity resulting from illness, necessity of work, and a variety of personal considerations. A second group included the students who were enrolled in programs such as engineering and veterinary medicine which require more than four years. About 35 per cent of those still in school after four years were in curricula with such requirements. The third group, about 45 per cent of those still in school after four years, had made a preference change sometime during their period in college which necessitated an extra quarter or possibly two in order to complete the degree.

These composite figures of students who either have graduated or have continued to progress satisfactorily toward a degree after four years are 46 per cent, 49 per cent, and 57 per cent. Recalling that this period covered the first three years of the Basic College, one might over-enthusiastically conclude that one indication of the effectiveness of the new program was to be found in the increased percentage of students completing a degree. As we shall see shortly, there were provisions in the Basic College program which encouraged students to remain in college when they might, under our former program, have discontinued. However, the period of time studied was just after the conclusion of World War II. In 1944 there were no veterans in the group admitted; in 1945, 5 per cent of the students were veterans, but in 1946, 68 per cent of them were veterans. We realized that maturity, financial status, and other attendant motivations of veterans must favorably affect the survival rate. Accordingly, we deliberately deferred until some later date, when the veteran group was out of college, a more careful study of the survival rate in relation to the Basic College advantages. In one way or another, however, veterans have continued, so that only in 1953 did we come to the point of making a really careful study of the problem again as a part of the previously-mentioned study by Warrington.

The Warrington study provides data which make interesting comparisons with those of Sheedy. These data are found in Table 16.

Striking an average over the three-year period, Sheedy arrived at the figure of 67 per cent of an entering class of students re-enrolling at the beginning of the third year. Warrington's data gave 61 per cent. If, however, the re-enrollment and the voluntary withdrawals with a C average or better are combined, the results of the two studies agree very closely at all points. The

TABLE 16

STUDENT MORTALITY AND SURVIVAL AT THE BEGINNING
OF THE THIRD YEAR AFTER ADMISSION

Status	Sheedy Study Average of 1944, 45, 46	Warrington Study 1953
Re-enrolling	67	61
Voluntary Withdrawal		
C Average or Above	10	16
Below C	15	14
Completed 2-year Terminal Program	2	2

reasons for more students with satisfactory records withdrawing
in the more recent study are not known. An increased transfer
rate because of more students enrolling in pre-professional programs and the possibility that more students are taking their
college program in pieces rather than as a four-year stint are the
most plausible explanations. Banzet's follow-up of withdrawals
showed that many students had definite intent of returning after
military service or the accumulation of some money.

Sheedy found that an additional 14 per cent of the students
discontinued in the last two years. Allowing for those still in
school, Sheedy estimated that 52 per cent of the starting group
has either completed their degrees by the end of four years or
very likely would do so within an additional year. In retrospect,
we can only wonder why we did not follow through for an additional year or two so that the report might be complete! Of the
48 per cent withdrawing prior to graduation approximately 38
per cent terminated voluntarily and the other 10 per cent were
dropped because of poor grades.

Sheedy's study refers explicitly to those completing a degree at

Michigan State. No estimate was available as to the number transferring to another college or professional school. At the end of the preceding chapter Banzet estimated that perhaps as high as 60 per cent of the entering group might ultimately complete a degree. Sheedy's figures (of which Banzet had full knowledge) are not inconsistent with this.

Warrington's figure of 61 per cent enrolled at the beginning of the third year makes the 60 per cent degree-acquiring estimate look rather more dubious. One feature of Warrington's data that provokes interest is the following:

	Re-entered Fall 1954	*Re-entered Fall 1955*
Men	73%	64%
Women	72%	57%

That this sex difference in survival is no accidental variation is borne out by another study involving a sample of students entering in 1951. For this sample, the readmission data in 1952 and 1953 yielded essentially the same results, except that the differential in favor of the men beginning the junior year was 9 per cent. The explanation of this sex differential is, we think, largely provided by two factors:

1. Withdrawal of girls who get married after two years of college;

2. Popularity among women of the two-year terminal courses in secretarial science.

Whether the Warrington data will ultimately yield the 60 per cent degree attainment figure that we have hypothesized is as yet uncertain. Short of a very careful and expensive follow-up of all withdrawals no accurate figure is possible, but should considerably less than 50 per cent complete their degree with us, we might need to revise our estimate of 60 per cent.

Salvage Operations

SURVIVAL THROUGH CHANGE

Prior to 1944, no freshman could enroll at Michigan State unless he declared at that time his choice among the available curricula. This practice, which is even yet a common one in higher education, was based on the assumption that individuals entering college knew—or should know—the field in which they wished to specialize. The truth of the matter was that many did not know what they wanted and chose a major on very inadequate grounds. A choice once made was not easily changed. The widespread feeling that the college freshman should know his own mind led to suspicion that one who wished to change was a poor risk. Poor grades attained because of disinterest, active dislike, or lack of aptitude rendered an applicant's acceptance in another program even more unlikely.

Often, the adviser in the initial program urged continuance with the original choice for another quarter on the grounds that the student would find himself or at least make sure that he was unsuited to that program. Another factor which operated to discourage changes in majors was the distinctiveness of many of the curricula. For example, engineering students had few courses in common with other fields. A student transferring into or out of engineering was almost certain to lose considerable credit, with the amount increasing rapidly with the length of his stay in college. Little wonder, then, that many students found it easier to withdraw from college than to change programs within it.

As one phase of the Basic College plan students were permitted to enroll as "no preference." Changes of preference within the first two years were made easy, and expert counseling assistance was provided for this purpose. The common core of Basic College courses also decreased the credit loss resulting from a change of preference. These features in the educational program made uncertainty and change in vocational plans both respectable and possible. In Chapter 12, Matteson reports on several aspects and results of the "no preference" and preference change procedure. Here we are concerned with the effect on student survival. It would be difficult to prove conclusively, but we are convinced that the new flexibility salvaged many students who would otherwise have withdrawn or been dropped. Here are our reasons for so thinking:

1. Provision of counseling assistance so that the undecided student could solve his indetermination at an early date helped to prevent the discouragement resulting from lack of purpose.
2. Students making initial choices on inadequate grounds were able to change with a minimum of red tape, although they were urged to think through the whole matter in one or more counseling interviews.
3. Wise preference changes improved the student's grade point averages, sometimes by amazing amounts. From a list, prepared at the close of a quarter, of students who had changed preference at the beginning of the quarter cases like the following are not unusual:

Grade Point Average Before Change	Grade Point Average After Change
1.56	3.20
1.82	2.64
2.75	4.00
1.00	2.60
1.50	2.00

It was estimated at one time, when nearly 30 per cent of the entering freshmen were declaring themselves as "no preference," that as high as 50 per cent of the graduating seniors had made a preference change. With elimination of some misuse of the system and the introduction of an extensive pre-enrollment summer counseling program, it is now doubtful that the per cent is quite that high. However, Warrington's study shows that of those freshmen entering in 1953 who completed two years, 38.1 per cent had made at least one preference change. Changes are relatively infrequent in the last two years, but it may be expected that further attrition (which we have found to be lower in the preference change group), terminal programs, and changes in preference of returning students will push the final figure to at least 40 per cent. Clearly students take advantage of the flexibility of our system and more graduate as a result of it.

THE COURT OF LAST RESORT

All educational institutions are faced with the problem of deciding when to drop the student whose grades are below whatever is considered a satisfactory performance. This decision is particularly critical when there is a distinction made between the first two and the last two years of work so that a definite action has to be taken in transferring each student from a lower to an upper division. At Michigan State no student is continued beyond the Basic College with less than a C average. Each year there are students who, after two years, are close to but still below the C average. Such students were originally given an additional quarter in the Basic College to make up their deficiency. If, in this additional quarter, the student either made no improvement or erased the deficiency there was no problem. However, some students improved but remained short of the required C average. A review of these cases suggested that many of the students on the one-term extension had not received as careful attention as might have been offered in planning their programs.[1]

One of the major difficulties was found when the unsatisfactory grades were received in one or two courses taken early in college in a major since rejected. For example, a student who started in engineering might have received failing grades in mechanical drawing and descriptive geometry but since have rejected that major and now be attempting to qualify for business administration. It seemed doubtful that low grades received in courses irrelevant to the student's present intention should keep him from continuing in college.

Although it was greeted with misgivings by some of the faculty, approval was given to a revised program. The first step involves more careful attention to all students granted a one-term extension. Each such person is advised to seek the services of the Counseling Center. There he is encouraged to re-examine his study habits, as well as his major and his purposes for being in college. He is also encouraged to repeat courses in which he incurred F or D grades, since raising such a course to a C is easier than taking new courses in which A's or B's must be obtained to balance F's or D's.

If after one quarter on the final-warning status, the student still has not achieved the C average for transfer but has definitely improved his status, he may be given a final-warning extension. This grants him a second term beyond the one in which he reached his junior status. Inauguration of this policy involves setting up categories labeled Final Warning I and Final Warning II. "Final" may now mean next to the last! During this second probationary term the student's records are referred to the college of his choice and an agreement is reached regarding credit not acceptable to that college. Any credits considered unacceptable for transfer are not counted toward graduation nor in the grade point average of the student by the college to which he wishes to transfer. If the student still does not achieve a C average with 92 or more quarter hour credits, he is asked to withdraw from the college.

THE ODDS ARE EVEN

In introducing this program providing for one more chance at achievement of academic respectability, it was planned that a study should be made of its effects. Table 17 shows the action on all students achieving junior status in the year 1951–52. Approximately 24 per cent of those reaching junior status did not immediately qualify for admission to an upper college.

TABLE 17

ACTIONS ON JUNIORS, 1951–52

	Transferred to Upper College	*Placed on Final Warning I*	*Placed on Final Warning II*
Fall 1951	509	148	95
Winter 1952	451	80	108
Spring 1952	1,094	161	45
Total	2,054	389	248

Of those students granted an additional term on Final Warning I, over the year 31 per cent of the Final Warning I students who continued qualified for continuance in their major after one additional quarter. Sixty-one per cent of those who continued in college made sufficient improvement that they were granted the second quarter under Final Warning II. Seven per cent were asked to withdraw.

As for the disposition of the Final Warning II students during the year, disregarding those students who voluntarily did not return, 55 per cent of the students qualified for the upper college at the end of the second probationary period and 45 per cent of them were withdrawn. In some respects, the phrase voluntary non-return is a misnomer, for in many cases the volition was that of a draft board.

A group of 123 juniors who qualified for an upper college after the second final-warning term tended to enter either the College of Science and Arts or the College of Business and Public Service. None changed colleges after they achieved admission, although some changed major within the college. The students as a group had below average academic aptitude. Whereas normal progress involved completion of the Basic College in six terms, this group averaged nine terms because of reduced programs, repetition of courses, and other irregularities.

As a group these students also tended, in their Basic College courses, to receive better grades from the instructor than on the common final examination. The improvement in their grades toward the end of their Basic College careers often seemed to result from enrollment in smaller and more advanced classes, where the role of examinations was minimized in determining grades. There would appear to be some basis for the student contention that he can surely graduate if he can only get by the first two years.

About 90 per cent of the students repeated courses to raise grades, averaging a repetition of 12 quarter hours per student. This repetition raised standing by an average of one and one-half points per credit repeated. Fifty-six per cent of the 123 students had some credits of unsatisfactory work deleted. The average number of credits thus dropped was 6, and this accounted for an average gain of 8 points toward the required C average.

At the close of winter quarter 1954, 82 per cent of the second final-warning group had either been graduated or were still in college making satisfactory progress. Only 3 per cent had been dropped, 15 per cent had discontinued (often for military service) although with satisfactory records. Making some allowance for probable returns of some of this group and including the students salvaged by the one-term extension, it is a reasonable estimate that 50 per cent of the students who reach the junior year with less than a C average can be salvaged and ultimately receive degrees.

The Graduates Talk Back

Naturally, we are concerned with reactions to the Basic College and its program. Whether the opinions obtained immediately after graduation are most suitable for appraising student reactions might be debated. Our feeling was that the new graduate has some perspective on his college experience, particularly the earlier part of it, which makes his reaction more objective, more perceptive, and less subject to distortion by trivialities than is true immediately after completing the courses. We feared that after a period away from the University, details of the first two years would become blurred and particular sources of satisfaction or dissatisfaction would be lost. Our compromise was to survey the graduates of three successive classes within a few weeks after receiving their degrees.

TO OUR TUNE

A questionnaire requesting certain reactions to Basic College courses, policies, and program was sent to all graduates of the classes of June 1954, June 1955, and June 1956. The rate of reply from the over 5,000 graduates was a little over 50 per cent. From the replies there were further deletions of those with incomplete responses, transfer students who entered as juniors, and of some highly irregular students. The graduates of the years 1954 and 1955 completed the Basic College requirements under the "old" seven-course program; those of 1956 completed requirements under the new four-course program. The simple one-page questionnaire to which these graduates responded is reproduced here. Each of the questions raised corresponded to some criticism or concern regarding the Basic College. The graduates were invited to use the back of the questionnaire for written comment.

REACTIONS TO BASIC COLLEGE COURSES

Background Information:
  1. Did you enter M.S.U. as a freshman?.............   Transfer............
  2. What Basic courses did you take?

Old Program:	New Program:
Written and	Communication
Spoken English	Skills ....
Physical Science	Natural Science ....
Social Science	Social Science ....
Biological Science...............	Humanities ....
Effective Living	

History of
Civilization ....
Literature & Fine
Arts ....

3. From what school did you graduate?

Agriculture................ Engineering................ Science and Arts................
   Home Economics................ Veterinary Medicine................
      Business Administration................ Education................

4. Sex: M................ F................   5. Year of birth................

Reactions:

1. How do you feel about the 45 hour credit requirement in Basic courses?

Too little................ About right................ Too much................

2. Check any of these values which you got from taking Basic courses.

No value at all ....   Practical infor-
General cultural   mation ....
background ....   Improved think-
Helped in select-   ing ability ....
ing major ....   Others (please
Developed some   list) :
new interests ....
Gained credit by
examination ....

3. How did the Basics compare with other courses in difficulty?

Less difficult................About the same................More difficult................

4. How did the quality of instruction in the Basics compare with that in your other courses?

Better................ About the same................ Not as good................

5. How did the examination in the Basics compare with those in other courses?

Better................ About the same................ Not as good................

6. Do you think that the forty-five hour requirement in Basics for general education should be continued?

Yes................   No................
  Because   Because
  Everyone needs   Some students
  this common   don't need them ....
  background   ....   Students should
  Freshmen don't   have more elec-
  know what they   tives   ....
  want   ....   Students need
  General educa-   more time for
  tion is needed on   majors   ....
  the job   ....   Other reasons:
  Other reasons:

7. How do you think that the professors in your major field felt about the Basic courses?

Favorable................   Indifferent................   Antagonistic................

8. Write any suggestions you have for improving the Basic courses on the back of this sheet.

With only roughly 50 per cent of the graduates replying, there may be some bias in the responses. In addition, there is some possibility that the questionnaire forces the graduate to "dance to our tune." The extent, however, to which the questions stimulated further response and the relevance of these to the questions raised indicated that we were successful in selecting key issues, and that the students were uninhibited in their response.

The Answers Are Clear

ABOUT THE 45 CREDIT GENERAL EDUCATION REQUIREMENT

Combining the students who felt the requirement to be too little and those who felt it to be about right, over 80 per cent of these graduates endorse the Basic College course requirements. The least favorable groups, Agriculture and Engineering, nevertheless gave better than a 70 per cent endorsement. Additional comments written in by these students indicated that a combination of the heavy major requirements and the deferral of their work caused by the Basic course requirements suggested a reduction in the requirements. Other Engineering and Agriculture graduates noted the same problem but were nevertheless insistent that the requirement be kept as the only way to insure some general education for these specialists.

THE VALUES OF THE BASICS

The most frequently noted value of the Basic courses is the provision of a general cultural background; this was checked by about 90 per cent of the graduates. The second rated value was that of developing some new interests, checked by over half of the graduates. Very close behind were the values of practical information and improved thinking ability. Only 5 to 10 per cent indicated that the Basics provided help in selecting their major, so that the interest-developing aspect of the Basics appears to be largely avocational.

The per cent of graduates who checked the "gained credit by examination" and who presumably gained some credit was 30 per cent in 1954, but decreased to 23 per cent in 1955 and 21 per cent in 1956. This reflects the tightening up on examination credit policies which is discussed by Mayhew and Warrington in Chapter 10.

The response "no value at all" was checked by 1 to 2 per cent of the graduates. This frank response deserves consideration even though coming from such a small percentage of the group. Among it are to be found some vocationally-minded students who want no part of general education. Included also are some individuals who did not meet the current standards for acquiring credit by examination but who felt, nonetheless, that the courses were highly repetitious of courses taken in high school. One may suspect here the confusion of casual familiarity with mastery.

This question as to the value of the Basic courses stimulated many of the graduates of the years 1954 and 1955 to remark on the changed course program of the Basic College. The most common comment was that reducing the seven courses to four would inevitably eliminate some of the most significant parts of the program. Concern was particularly manifested about the probable de-emphasis on the areas of art, literature, and music. Many students expressed regret at the elimination of all choice in the program.

DIFFICULTY OF THE BASICS

The graduates were about equally divided between regarding the Basics as of the same difficulty as their other courses and as of lesser difficulty. Only about 15 per cent—mostly women and elementary education majors—found them more difficult. Engineering graduates tended to find the Basics easier, or so 70 per cent of them said.

The graduates under the new program, by about a 5 per cent margin as compared with the earlier classes taking the old Basics, list the Basics as of equal difficulty with their other courses. Whether this results from a real increase in difficulty, from the increase from 3 to 4 credits for three of the courses, or from other unrecognized factors is unknown. In general, the spread of opinions and the loading of them suggest that the Basics are well adjusted to their purposes and the level at which they are offered. We should not want them to be "snaps" but we should fail in our purpose if they were harder than the courses required in the various major fields. The elementary education group has for several years been one of the lowest ranking groups in ability and their reaction is, therefore, not surprising.

QUALITY OF INSTRUCTION

Approximately 55 per cent of each of the groups of graduates considered the quality of instruction in the Basics about the same as that found in their other courses. Only about 10 per cent rated Basic instruction as better and the remainder, about 35 per cent, regarded it as not as good. Considering that the Basics are required and that large numbers of instructors are involved, the response is generally favorable. Those who checked the Basic instruction as "not as good" often supplied a comment. The most common ones were:

1. Some teachers aren't interested in the Basic courses and do not try to interest their students.

2. The courses attempt to cover too much in too little time.

3. The material does not challenge the superior student.

4. Some teachers lack background in certain aspects of the Basic course which they teach and consequently bore or antagonize students.

BASIC COLLEGE EXAMINATIONS

Over half (53%) of the graduates felt that the Basic course examinations were inferior to the others they experienced and only 10–15 per cent regarded them as better. This strong and consistent reaction to both the old comprehensive and the more recent term examination results from several factors which we can extract from the written comments. Some of the students do not like objective tests and some do not like the weight attached to them in determination of the final grade. The central objection, however, is that the examinations are ambiguous—guessing games or intelligence tests rather than tests of what is covered in the course.

Only a few students are perceptive enough to recognize the deliberate intent in the examination to pose a question in a new guise or to require an application or a relating of ideas rather than recall. Such questions are somewhat more difficult, but the real problem is that many of the students do not realize that these are reasonable tasks, both appropriate and amenable to reason. Somehow, in our courses we have failed to direct the attention of some students beyond the specific facts to the underlying concepts and principles, and to the applicability of these to a wide range of situations and problems. It is not surprising that it is so; it is a difficult task.

It is easy to rationalize away unpleasant evidence rather than to face up to it. We are convinced that the reactions of these graduates to our examinations should not be ignored. We, too, are less than completely satisfied with our examinations, but the correction of our dissatisfaction would result in more emphasis on thought and cause more dissatisfaction with students. We do better at talking about thinking and at developing questions that might evoke it, than we do at making students realize that this is an objective and at stimulating them to improve their thinking. The evidence is clear on this point in the values which they ascribe to the Basic courses. Cultural background (facts) appeals to over 90 per cent; but 50 per cent or less admit to gaining improved thinking ability.

CONTINUATION OF THE 45 HOUR REQUIREMENT

As might be expected from the earlier data, 85 per cent of the graduates indicate that the 45 hour requirement should be continued. The need for this common background is checked as a reason by 70 per cent and the importance of general education on the job is checked by 60 per cent. Only 16 to 20 per cent felt that the indecision of the freshmen would be a justification for the requirement. Those who felt the requirement should not be continued were concerned only with some reduction in hours which would permit more electives or more time for the major.

ATTITUDE OF MAJOR FIELD PROFESSORS

This element was introduced into the questionnaire because there had been some reports of prejudicial comments to students about the Basic courses. Over the three-year period there has been a trend toward increasingly favorable response on this student judgment of professor attitude. The per cent of students checking a favorable attitude for their professors has increased from 40 to 44 per cent and, at the same time, the per cent of unfavorable decreased from 11 to 8. For engineering graduates the per cent checking a favorable response rose from 21 per cent to 44 per cent while the antagonistic response decreased from 17 per cent to 6 per cent. The extensive use of the indifference response suggests that many students found no basis for judgment. At the least, the responses show that few major professors, whatever may be their opinion, speak slightingly of the Basics to their advisees. We should add that there is no reason to believe that many ever did so.

And They Have Ideas Too

The graduates were invited to write comments on the back of the questionnaire and many of them did so. These comments generally indicated a real desire to be of help; they were neither carping, unreasoned criticisms nor were they superficial and meaningless encomiums. Many admitted that they did not really appreciate the Basic College program until some time after they completed it. Some students felt that some of the work was repetitious and that not enough provision is made for the superior student. Several suggested careful screening by initial testing so that the courses could be better adapted to the level of the students without excusing any from them. Several made comments along lines by no means suggested by the questionnaire. Thus one argued that the Basic courses create more contact among freshmen from all fields and provide thereby a wider circle of friends than would otherwise be the case. Another commented that the Basic courses greatly eased the transition period from high school to college, particularly for the "just average" student.

Many made the pertinent comment that the value of the courses depended very much on the instructors that one had. Every course came in for criticism and every one came in for praise. Practically every point of criticism by one graduate was the basis of praise by another. In some cases this may have been the result of differing viewpoints, but in many cases it was the result of having different teachers.

The reactions of our graduates are so clear that no elaborate summary is necessary. In retrospect they have considerable insight into the reasons for the existence of the Basic College and the Basic course requirements. By an overwhelming majority they favor the idea. Their criticism is, with few exceptions, given with understanding and insight. We can see in their criticisms short-comings which we have also recognized. It is not easy to over-come them because the really significant shortcomings involve matters of classroom instruction and of the learning process about which we know too little and upon which even deans and depart-ment heads have little direct influence.

Note

[1] Joseph Sheedy and Paul L. Dressel, "The Effect of a Final Warning Extension on Academic Performance," *College and University*, October 1955, pp. 48–52.

Part III

ABOUT
OUR
EXAMINATIONS

7

ROBERT A. JACKSON

In the Beginning

There Are Always Tests

The new student at any American college is likely to be greeted by a battery of examinations. He may have taken an examination some months before to qualify for admission. If he is a scholarship recipient, it is likely that an examination was required as a basis for that award. With increasing enrollments, examinations have an ever-weightier role in the grading of students. Fortunately, most students are inured to tests because of the extensive use of them in the elementary and secondary schools. For some students, however, formal testing situations continue to be a distracting experience. At one point in our concern with student withdrawals, we found that our programming of tests on the first day of the orientation period without adequate prior contact and explanation of the program resulted in some individuals returning home, convinced by the ordeal that they should not be in college. In some cases, their snap judgment may have been appropriate, but we did modify our program to alleviate this situation. Tests are more valid and present a less frightening task when their purposes are understood by those who take them.

This chapter presents some of the data obtained from the orientation test program, which includes 1) the basic test battery —a test of scholastic aptitude, a reading test, and achievement tests in English and arithmetic; and 2) special tests administered to provide data pertinent to various aspects of the college program.

The basic test data for each student are made available to various administrative officials, all departments, and the college counselors. The data are available to students only through counselors and enrollment officers. The test results have also been used in studies of admission problems, prediction of academic success, and changing ability level in a sequence course.

The special tests, which are usually changed from year to year, are used to investigate pertinent aspects of the Basic College program. Two major topics investigated in this manner were 1) status of new students relative to the material covered in a Basic course; and 2) amount of gain in content objectives as a result of completing three terms of a Basic course.

The Orientation Test Battery as an Admission Device

Any student not meeting the normal admission requirements of Michigan State is permitted to apply for admission by examination. For many years the orientation test battery was used to assess the aptitude of such a student for college. The applicant's performance on these examinations and his previous record (scholastic and experience) were used to judge his qualifications for admission. The individuals were then placed in one of three groups:

1. Passing—admitted as regular student by virtue of performing as well or better than the average student admitted by the normal admission procedure.

2. Failing—not admitted.

3. Summer school trial—admitted on a trial basis to summer school and, if work is satisfactory, admitted as a regular student. Such admissions were restricted to those who came close to achieving the passing standard.

Between February 1949 and March 1950, entrance examinations were administered to 742 applicants. This group was chosen for detailed study. Less than one-third of those taking the exami-

nations passed them; approximately 90 per cent of those passing
the examinations entered Michigan State. Included in the 742
cases were 82 who had previously failed the examinations; approximately 25 per cent were successful on the second trial.

It is easy to determine whether those students who passed the
examinations succeeded in college, but it is also necessary to
determine whether students who failed could have succeeded in
college. Therefore, the decision was made in the summer of 1949
to admit some of the failures as regular students in the fall
quarter of 1949. These students were not told that they had
failed, but were simply notified of their admission. The study
included 209 individuals who passed the examinations, 123 who
failed, and 40 summer school trial students. At the time of this
study the pass and fail groups had completed, on the average,
three terms of college work; the summer school trial group, three
and one-half terms. The students were classified according to
their records as average or above, below average but passing, and
withdrew or withdrawn due to failing grades. The percentages of
each examination group within each grade point group are given
in Table 18.

TABLE 18

PERCENTAGE OF EACH EXAMINATION GROUP
WITHIN INDICATED GRADE POINT GROUP

| | *Examination Group* | | |
| *Grade Point Classification* | | | *Summer School* |
	Passing	*Failing*	*Trial*
Average or Above	56.5	13.0	50.0
Below Average but Passing	28.7	46.4	30.0
Failing	14.8	40.6	20.0

The relative success of the three groups was generally consistent with their performance on the entrance examinations. The

best academic grade point average achieved in the failing group was C+. The three students attaining this average were veterans and older than the usual freshman. We concluded that:

1. The test battery did rather adequately distinguish, in this special group of doubtful admissions prospects, between students who had the ability to do college work and those who did not.

2. The 14.8 per cent of the students who passed the examinations but failed to succeed in college was consistent with the general percentage of attrition in the college program. This suggested that the standards used were appropriate.

On statistical grounds we had reason to be satisfied with this use of tests as an auxiliary admissions procedure. However, a by-product of our study resulted in complete alteration of the program. Students who came to the campus, took the tests, and then, after a lapse of several days, received word of their rejection were unhappy about it. So were their parents. We decided that a more individualized procedure involving the counseling staff would permit more careful assessment of the personality and motivation of the individual, a wiser selection of tests based upon his particular plans, and an opportunity to develop with the individual other appropriate possibilities when admission was inappropriate. This program, discussed by Matteson in Chapter 12, proved equally effective in admitting the right students and much more effective in helping those not admitted to formulate other plans.

The Orientation Test Battery as a Predictive Device

Almost every college has buried somewhere in its files at least one study devoted to the prediction of academic success. There are literally hundreds of studies each year on the relationship between tests and college grades. Although such data are not as useful as the researcher expects, it is desirable to know the extent of relationship between college grades and orientation tests. We report here one of many such studies of the relationship between tests and first-term grade point average.

The individuals in this study were first-term freshmen in the fall term of 1952. Only those students carrying a full college load (from 12 to 19 credit hours) were included. All had completed the following four tests:

1. ACE Psychological Examination developed by the Educational Testing Service.

2. Michigan State College Reading Test constructed by the Board of Examiners.

3. Tests of English Usage, Third Edition, constructed by Benjamin B. Hickok of the Department of Communication Skills in cooperation with the Board of Examiners.

4. Arithmetic Proficiency Test constructed by the staff of the Arithmetic Improvement Service.

SEX DIFFERENCES

Of the 3,053 freshmen tested during orientation week, 2,983 completed one term of college work; the other 70 students withdrew from college with no college grades. Since it was known that the mean grade point average of the women was significantly higher than that of the men, the students were divided on the basis of sex. The means, standard deviations, and intercorrelations of the five variables were obtained for the 1,687 men and the 1,296 women completing one term of college work; they are given in Tables 19 and 20. The scores on the four tests are derived scores based on a 10-point scale; the grade average is calculated in the usual manner, with A assigned the value 4 down to F with the value 0.

Tests of statistical significance were applied to the data given in Tables 19 and 20, and these conclusions were apparent:

1. Freshman men have a significantly higher mean on the Arithmetic Test than do the freshman women.

2. Freshman women have significantly higher means on the English Test and the Reading Test than do the freshman men.

3. Freshman women have a significantly higher mean grade point average than do the freshman men.

4. The means of the men and women on the Psychological Test are not significantly different.

TABLE 19

MEAN AND STANDARD DEVIATIONS ON THE INDICATED
VARIABLES FOR MEN AND WOMEN

Variable	*Mean*		*Standard Deviation*	
	Men	*Women*	*Men*	*Women*
Grade Point Average	2.2	2.4	.70	.68
Psychological Examination	5.4	5.3	1.71	1.65
Reading Examination	5.2	5.5	1.70	1.64
English Examination	4.9	6.1	1.64	1.56
Arithmetic Examination	5.6	5.0	1.68	1.61

TABLE 20

INTERCORRELATIONS BETWEEN THE INDICATED VARIABLES
(Values above the diagonal are for men; those below for women.)

	Grade Pt. Average	*Psych. Exam.*	*Read. Exam.*	*Eng. Exam.*	*Arith. Exam.*
Grade Point Average		.43	.50	.49	.46
Psychological Examination	.52		.74	.56	.47
Reading Examination	.64	.74		.59	.39
English Examination	.52	.60	.61		.44
Arithmetic Examination	.42	.49	.42	.46	

5. The best predictor of grade point average is the Reading Test.

The multiple regression approach with two or more variables yielded no better prediction of success than the Reading Test alone. This same result has been confirmed by several similar correlation studies. The preceding data and other knowledge about the four tests indicated the desirability of restricting further investigation to the Psychological Test and Reading Test.

LOAD AND ACHIEVEMENT

The next part of this investigation was concerned with the relationship between grade point average and number of credits carried. The individuals in each of the sex groups were further classified into eight subgroups according to the number of credits carried. The analysis of variance technique was used to test differences in group means. The data are not presented here but they indicated that the mean grade point average increased regularly with an increased credit load. The mean score on both the Psychological Test and the Reading Test also increased with credit load. The analysis of covariance technique was next used to adjust grade point averages on the basis of Reading Test scores. The adjusted mean grade point averages were still significantly different but at a much lower level of significance than the unadjusted grade point average means. This suggested one of the major causes of differences in mean grade point average to be differences in reading ability; however, other factors are operating so as to cause the adjusted mean grade point average to increase with credit load. Students taking heavier credit loads are generally more able and more highly-motivated students and continue to perform at the expected higher level despite the heavier load.

EARLY DROPOUTS

The mean scores on the Psychological and Reading Tests for those men completing the one term and for those withdrawing during the first term, and similar data for the women indicate that the men who withdrew during the first quarter had a somewhat lower mean score on both of the tests than the group completing one term. The women withdrawing from school during the first term had mean Reading and Psychological Test scores nearly identical with the mean scores of those completing one term. Of the freshmen tested during orientation week, 2.8 per cent of the men and 1.7 per cent of the women withdrew during their first quarter. Apparently lack of ability is not the major factor operative in causing these withdrawals.

POINT AVERAGE EXPECTANCY TABLES

Correlations between test scores and grade point averages have already been given but these are rather difficult to use directly. A second method of analyzing the relationship between grade point average and test scores involves the computation of the probability that a person with a given score on a predictor will achieve various grade levels. This method helps to communicate to an individual his probability of doing at least as well as certain cutoff points on the criterion.

Since the critical point is a C average, it seemed desirable to determine the chances of various students doing at least average work in their first term of college. Since after the first quarter of college an individual's grade point average might be unrepresentative of his eventual grade point average, the grade point scale was dichotomized into upper and lower groups at a grade point average of 1.75. The lower group included 23 per cent of the men and 16 per cent of the women.

The students were also divided into three levels of ability by orientation test scores. Thus the success of high, middle, and low ability students in attaining a C average could be determined. As expected, one can be almost certain that the high ability student will do satisfactorily in his first term, but there is about a 50–50 chance that the low ability student may also make the grade.

To present such information in a form more useful in a

counseling situation, expectancy tables were constructed to show the chances of achieving various grade point averages. Tables 21 and 22 were constructed on the basis of the empirical data contained in this study.

TABLE 21

PERCENTAGE OF MEN WITH A GIVEN DERIVED SCORE ON THE
READING TEST MAKING A GRADE POINT AVERAGE AT OR ABOVE
THE INDICATED GRADE POINT AVERAGE

Grade Point Average	Reading Examination Derived Score									
	1	2	3	4	5	6	7	8	9	10
3.75							3	9	9	17
3.25				1	4	8	17	27	46	43
2.75	9	2	3	6	19	29	39	50	71	83
2.25	23	18	17	31	47	61	73	82	86	92
1.75	45	41	52	65	79	87	93	96	100	92
1.25	68	73	83	88	95	95	98	98		92

TABLE 22

PERCENTAGE OF WOMEN WITH A GIVEN DERIVED SCORE ON THE
READING TEST MAKING A GRADE POINT AVERAGE AT OR ABOVE
THE INDICATED GRADE POINT AVERAGE

Grade Point Average	Reading Examination Derived Score									
	1	2	3	4	5	6	7	8	9	10
3.75						1	2	11	19	10
3.25			1	1	2	8	23	42	54	20
2.75	14		2	9	15	29	54	71	84	100
2.25	29	7	23	39	51	66	81	92	97	
1.75	43	37	52	76	81	93	96	99	100	
1.25	72	93	82	92	96	99	98	100		

The cell entries in each of the columns are cumulative, telling the chances of reaching or exceeding the indicated grade point average. Each table shows, for a particular derived-score group on the predictor, the chances in one hundred of achieving a certain grade point average or better. Table 21, for example, suggests that 52 per cent of the men with a derived score of 3 on the Reading Test will obtain a grade point average of 1.75 or better, and that ninety-six per cent of those with derived scores of 8 will perform in the same manner.

It should be remembered that a student's grade point average depends on his interests, motivation, and other important factors not measured by tests. The average achievement of students with a particular derived score is not indicative of what is appropriate for a particular person. Furthermore, the following limitations should be kept in mind:

1. Each derived score has an error of measurement; thus, the true score for a particular individual on one of the tests might be 6 rather than his observed score of 5, or 4 rather than 5.

2. The grade point average is based on one quarter of work; a particular student's grade point average may not be representative of the total grade point average he will eventually compile.

3. The probabilities presented are based on group performance, and do not necessarily hold for individual prediction.

COURSE GRADES AND ORIENTATION TESTS

The preceding study was concerned with the use of the orientation test battery as a predictor of first-term grade point average. From time to time other studies have been undertaken to determine the relationship between the Psychological Examination and the Reading Test and grades in individual college courses. In one such study, undertaken primarily to determine the relative value of the Quantitative and Linguistic subscores on the ACE Psychological Examination, Dressel[1] found the Linguistic score above almost as effective as the total score for prediction in most courses. Correlations of the total score were highest with Social Science grades (.57 for women, .63 for men). In most cases the correlations were higher for women than for men.

The majority of our studies involved the Basic College courses. Correlation coefficients for each of the Basic courses were obtained between the comprehensive examination grade and the following variables: 1) ACE Psychological Examination, 2) Michigan State College Reading Test, and 3) Term grades. As usual, the correlations were higher for women than for men, although we have not dared to conclude that women are more predictable than men. The correlations between year-end comprehensive examination grades and orientation test scores were lower than the correlations between term grades and comprehensive grades. One would reasonably expect this, since the best predictor in an academic field is previous performance in that field. Under the revised system, involving both instructor and examination grades, the orientation test scores are found to correlate more highly with the examination than with the instructor. The Reading Test is consistently a better predicting device than the Psychological Examination.

Changing Ability Level in a Sequence Course

An early and recurring criticism of the program of acceleration in the Basic courses was that the net effect was to sift out the more able individuals, thereby decreasing the ability level of students from the first through the third quarter of each Basic. The situation was more complex than the casual critics realized. The ability of groups enrolled in successive quarters of a sequence course is the result of a number of selective factors.

Student withdrawals take place in all ranges of ability, but they are heaviest among the less able. The effect of student withdrawal, then, is to give a gradually increasing level of ability in a sequence course. An extensive acceleration program of credit by examination, in contrast with withdrawal, draws primarily from the higher levels of ability. The composite effect of these two major selection factors could be known only by accumulation of data.

The students completing the first term of all Basic courses in the fall of 1947 were selected for study. For every student we had available the score on the American Council on Education Psychological Examination and the Cooperative Reading Test. One indication of the changes in the group relative to ability is shown by comparing the average score on the ACE Psychological Examination and the Cooperative Reading Test for students completing one term of the course and those completing three terms of the courses. Comparison of term 1 with term 3 averages showed a small but consistent decrease in the ability level of the groups except in the course with the smallest amount of acceleration, which showed higher average ability at the end of the three terms than in the first term.

To further study the changing complexion of the group ability level throughout the year, students were divided into three ability groups on the basis of their Psychological Test deciles as follows: High (H)—decile score of 10, 9, 8; Average (M)—decile score of 7, 6, 5, 4; and Low (L)—decile score of 3, 2, 1.

Of an entering group of new students, 30 per cent would be in the high and low groups and 40 per cent in the average group. Over all Basic courses the 30-40-30 distribution characterized the fall group, and by the end of spring term the distribution was changed to 27-43-30. In science, for example, 23 per cent of the high group passed the examination early while 18 per cent of the high group withdrew, a total loss of 41 per cent of the high group from fall to spring. At the same time, however, 45 per cent of the low group had also disappeared. The net effect was little change. However, without acceleration, the spring term group would definitely have been a more able group than that of the fall. From these facts, which are almost irrelevant to deciding on the actual worth of acceleration, one can argue either pro or con on its effects, depending on his attitude toward it.

One result of these investigations was the thought of modifying the grade distribution for a course on the basis of the ability level of the group completing the course, *i.e.*, a larger percentage of A's and B's would be given to a group with a higher than average ability level. An obvious objection to this procedure is that achievement does not always parallel ability. The data definitely indicated that the use of a fixed grade distribution for all of the Basic courses would not be desirable. However, the final conclusion was that the percentage limits and policies for the grade distribution were sufficiently liberal to permit percentage variations appropriate to a superior or inferior group.

Student Backgrounds in the Basic Courses

To effectively evaluate the Basic College program it was desirable to have information on the background of the students relative to a Basic course at the time of first enrollment in the course. To secure some data on this topic, two research projects were undertaken.

Comprehensive examinations of the previous spring were administered to a group of new students to determine their status relative to the Basic courses at the time of their entering college. Each of the seven comprehensive examinations was administered to different groups of 300–400 new freshman students in the fall of 1948. Thus, these students faced the same task as the students completing three terms of the corresponding Basic courses.

Admittedly the psychological aspects of the situation are different. The students who have completed the course have some familiarity with the materials and have some degree of motivation since their grade depended on the performance. Entering students know relatively less about an area and possibly lack motivation. Recognizing this, but lacking more precise information, the obtained data would seem to be as reliable as any information available on the status of new freshman students relative to the Basic courses. The percentages of the freshmen attaining various grade levels on the comprehensive examination, as determined by standards used with students completing the course, are given in Table 23.

These data show considerable variation in the backgrounds of students for the different courses. Based on the objective portion

TABLE 23

PERCENTAGE OF ENTERING FRESHMEN ATTAINING VARIOUS GRADES
ON COMPREHENSIVE EXAMINATIONS

Course	A	B	C	D	F
Written and Spoken English	0.8	6.4	35.4	36.4	21.0
Biological Science	0.0	0.0	6.9	15.7	77.4
Physical Science	0.0	0.6	8.7	24.6	66.2
Social Science	0.0	0.7	8.9	18.5	71.8
Effective Living	0.0	0.0	2.5	12.6	84.9
History of Civilization	0.0	0.6	0.9	6.8	91.8
Literature and Fine Arts	0.0	0.0	0.3	0.6	99.1

of the English examination (a speech and a theme being omitted) nearly 43 per cent of the freshman group tested would have made a C or better. In Literature and Fine Arts, the percentage drops to less than one-half of one per cent. In general the data indicated that the Basic courses were set at such a level that few students have a mastery of the course at the time of admission. However, when one considers the fact that the examinations were given without warning, it seemed reasonable to expect that possibly 10 per cent of the students enrolling in a Basic course are capable of achieving a C or better on an examination with only a limited amount of preparation. Indeed, our experience would suggest that if this is not true the course is improperly adjusted to the students.

It should be recalled here that the entire curriculum has been revised since the date of this study. Nonetheless, the study suggests the advisability of either some special sections in each Basic course providing a quick over-view of the entire course for the more capable students or some enriched sections for the more capable students rather than the more common practice of enrolling all students in the first quarter of a sequence course. It also seems necessary to have some type of pre-testing to identify the more

capable students in each course. The problems of large enrollments have militated against such procedures, but interest continues and in two courses there are such provisions.

The Effects of the Basic Courses

In an attempt to determine the amount of gain made by
students in content objectives, the Basic College Evaluation Committee decided to give a pre-test to all freshmen and to follow up
with a post-test on the same items after completion of a Basic
course. The Office of Evaluation Services was requested to develop an examination which would provide a reliable index of
group status, although not of individual status, relative to each
Basic course. The items were selected or written by the examiners
and reviewed by the appropriate department with the following
principles in mind:

1. The items should be largely from old examinations and
should have demonstrated appropriate difficulty and high discrimination.

2. The items, so far as possible, should constitute a representative sample of the course material.

3. The items for Part I of the pre-test should measure knowledge or understanding of facts, concepts, and principles; those
for Part II should involve application of some form of critical
thinking.

The extent to which these criteria were met in the selection of
the items varied somewhat. Certain types of material used in a
regular comprehensive examination were omitted because they
could not be easily administered to a group of freshmen. In the
communications area it was not possible to obtain theme and
speech ratings so that all the evidence is on the basis of the objective portion of the examination.

The pre-test data were obtained by administering the test to
entering students in the fall of 1947 as a special part of the orientation test battery. Some of the necessary post-test data was obtained by including the pre-test items identified with a specific

course in the comprehensive examination for that course the following spring. In each course, 100 students were selected to cover the full range of achievement as measured by the total examination. This group, known as the experimental group, consisted of 100 students who had taken the pre-test in the fall, completed three terms of the course, and repeated the same items at the end of the course. For each of the students two scores were computed, the first being the number of items answered correctly in the fall, and the second being the number answered correctly in the spring.

A second group of 100 students—all of whom had taken the pre-tests in the fall—was randomly selected to repeat the pre-test items for a Basic course that they had not been enrolled in. For each student, two similar scores were obtained. Data from this group, designated as the control group, would provide an indication of gain made in a particular course area when not enrolled in the course. No control group was available for the communications course since it is required of all freshmen.

In arriving at conclusions on the basis of the data, it seemed desirable to obtain an average pre-test score and an average post-test score for each group. These averages were expressed as a percentage of the total number of items in the test. With the data in this form and a sample of only 100, some caution was necessary in interpreting the data. The pre-test percentages indicated rather clearly that students do not begin any of the Basic courses with complete ignorance of the material included in the course. The students initially answered 30 to 50 per cent of the pre-test items for the various courses.

An index of gain was obtained by taking the difference between the post-test per cent and the pre-test per cent. The gains registered by the control groups were generally small (5 to 10%); this indicated that through maturation or from some related courses students made some improvement in Basic course areas without formal training. The gains for the experimental groups (25 to 30%) were significantly larger than the gains for the control groups. A further study of gains was made by classifying each student of the experimental group according to his grade in the comprehensive examination. The results indicated that the students with the larger pre-test scores made the greater gain and obtained the higher grades.

Summary

Even the person most unsympathetic to research will admit that we know more about our students as a result of such studies as these. The extent to which the results affect practice is something else. The studies on initial status and on gains in the Basic courses were made some years ago; the fact that they have not been repeated in recent years is reasonably good evidence that faculty interest is not widespread. Nevertheless, the facts revealed have influenced the thinking of numerous individuals. For example, no one can look at the data on gains over the Basic courses and still believe that students begin a course with no knowledge and master a minimum of 70 per cent in order to receive credit for the course.

Perhaps this modification of preconceptions must be considered as the most tangible outcome. Changing conditions, however, require re-study of earlier generalizations and statistics. For example, the development of extensive remedial services resulted in lowered correlations between orientation test scores and grades. The extent to which such correlations are lowered might be regarded as an index of the effectiveness of the remedial services in enabling the student to remove the disabilities revealed by tests. Only as such statistics are made routinely available can their sensitivity and significance in planning and understanding an education program be properly appraised.

Note

[1] Ralph Berdie, Paul Dressel, and Paul Kelso, "Relative Validity of the Q and L Scores on the ACE Psychological Examination," *Educational & Psychological Measurement,* Winter 1951, pp. 803–812.

8

PART 1.   OSMOND E. PALMER
PART 2.   CLARENCE H. NELSON

In Courses of Course

Introduction

The preparation of examinations in the Basic courses has been the responsibility of the Board of Examiners. Naturally, much attention has been given to improvement of the examinations. At one time this took the direction of extensive statistical analysis such as item analyses, computation of reliability, correlation of examination grades and theme and speech ratings with other evidence of achievement, and the like. We soon found that statistical reliability had little to do with the extent to which teachers would rely on the test and value the results. Our attention has turned to developing examinations more in accord with the avowed purposes of our teachers, who require something more than factual recall, and who try to encourage more learning and self-evaluation on the part of the students. Accordingly, this chapter summarizes two quite different aspects of our thinking and study in the attempt to improve our course examinations.

The first aspect relates experiences in arriving at a "satisfactory" procedure for rating themes and speeches. While this task is now of less importance—since themes and speeches are now required only for the accelerating students—the insights achieved continue to be helpful. Evaluation of written and oral materials does involve somewhat different problems than objective testing. The changing group of instructors necessitates continued re-study and revision of policies and procedures.

The second aspect of our thinking about examinations involves studies of student thought processes on examinations and attempts to develop and study novel testing situations of objective nature.

Part 1—Rating Themes and Speeches

Originally the Written and Spoken English (now Communication Skills) final examination determined the student's grade for a whole year's work. In a skills course stressing writing and speaking, it was obviously necessary to include a speech and theme. In spite of some fear of the task, they decided that each student should write a paper and give a speech. Ultimately, each instructor had to judge speeches for about forty hours during the last week of the course and to read as many as 120 extra papers during the last two weeks.

The situation raised these problems:

1. What sort of a task could be set which would permit students to demonstrate in two hours the qualities which we expected in speaking and writing?

2. How could we systematize the evaluation by two or three raters of a given performance?

3. As more and more people were involved in the ratings, what could be done to define standards which would be used by all?

4. An insolvable problem was the factor of fatigue and rush in the last two weeks of a term. Even with good will a person might not rate speeches late in the day as he did in the morning; he might not rate a set of themes well after judging speeches all day.

From quarter to quarter we worked at each of these problems (except the last) but we spent most of our time in achieving more uniform ratings. This was important not only for grades but in our work in class from day to day. In this chapter we begin with a discussion of problems connected with theme rating, and turn to speech rating more briefly, usually pointing out only those ways in which the speech problems and solutions were different.

THE SUBJECT FOR THE WRITING ASSIGNMENT

In the choice of topics there were two criteria. The first was that the topic elicit the type of performance we wanted, and the second was that it be something the student could handle adequately under examination conditions. We were never sure that we reconciled these two requirements.

For both speech and theme, we originally produced booklets containing a miscellany of data on a subject which we hoped would provide the student with a foundation for developing his ideas. Unfortunately, the number of specific topics needed was numerous because we wanted a different topic each day of the week so that a student could not anticipate his exact task. We wanted enough different speech topics so that no two students would talk on the same one during the same period. The various topics, it turned out, were unequal in difficulty. For some topics the booklets were adequate; for others they were not. In the theme-rating situation there was another problem. A rater might begin a paper without realizing that the topic being developed was slightly different from that in the paper he had just read. Occasionally a rater could not discern which of five topics a student was writing about.

We decided to have all students meet on one or two evenings to write their papers. This meant that they would all be writing on two topics at most. We tried giving the students a 500-word discussion of a topic and then asking them to write on some aspect of it. Too often the student tended only to paraphrase what he read. A variation of this was to give the student a series of headlines followed by a specific problem. The headlines, we hoped, would serve as reminders of something he had seen or read without suggesting an organization and without giving him solid chunks of matter which he could paraphrase.

Generally, the staff demanded that a subject be broad and brief. Many of them feel that the student should have to narrow the subject, work out an organization, and find his own content.

We tried topics like "Communications" or "Politics," but the resulting papers could hardly be judged by the same yardstick. One paper gave rise to a lot of discussion. With the problem "Communications" before him, a Korean veteran wrote about a radio center in the Pacific. It was a well-written and vivid paper but it grew out of the assigned topic only vaguely; it did not solve any problem of limiting or of organization and went little beyond simple narration. It could be graded high and was. But it was not the kind of job we wanted.

One other type of topic we tried when we thought it part of our job to teach a little about the reading of graphs and statistics. We gave the students a real estate map of a town, indicating residential areas, business areas, industry, schools, churches, etc. We also gave them some data about location, job opportunities, town income, size of school budget, and the like. We asked the student to tell why he would (or would not) like to live in this town. Then we had great argument about how to mark a paper the gist of which was: I would not like to live there because it is "dry" and I like to drink.

Obviously, the subjective appraisal by raters of the satisfactoriness of a theme topic has not led us in any definite direction. The alternative of studying the performance of the students on different topics is complicated by the factor of reader reliability, about which we will shortly say a great deal.

THE SUBJECTS FOR SPEAKING

The speech topics for a number of years were relatively stable. Since most of our students were taking two or three other Basics while they were taking Written and Spoken English, we had an opportunity to have the students speak on something about which they had specific information. With the help of staff members of the other Basics, we devised a set of speech topics for each course. In Biological Science, for instance, we had an area "Characteristics Common to All Living Things," and thirteen specific topics in that area, such as "The Basic of Life—the Cell" and "The Role of Water in Life." The student would choose one of these areas several weeks before the date of the test. When he came to the examination, he brought with him notes, texts, and anything else he liked. Then, after he had chosen one of three of the specific topics in the area, he was given half an hour in which to organize his thinking and to find any specific data he wished to use for accuracy or illustration.

This type of speech subject we used for a number of years. Many of the topics produced top-notch speeches, particularly in Biological Science. In some of the areas where the material was difficult we got little more than a trite rehash of textbook stuff. However, in comparison with theme topics, we seemed here to have hit upon as satisfactory a solution as possible.

There was some feeling, particularly on the part of the staff of the Physical Science course, that the scientifically untrained teachers of Written and Spoken English were letting those students who spoke on scientific topics get by with a lot of errors. One term five or six Physical Science instructors accepted an invitation to judge a dozen or so speeches each. Uniformly they rated the students higher in content than did the three Written and Spoken English instructors in the room!

With the change in the Basic College from seven courses to four, this type of topic became less usable. All students, or nearly all, would be taking only one other Basic, Natural Science; one-third might be taking Social Science; practically none would be in Humanities. The decisive factor in dropping these speech topics was that now only special permission students (those trying to pass one or two terms of the course by examination) are required to give speeches. These, it was agreed, should be required to give a persuasive speech, whereas the topics in the Basics lent themselves better to exposition.

At the moment, we have a set of topics consisting of controversial statements, or half-truths, which a student can attack or defend, in part or *in toto*. Examples of these are "Our education will improve only when we put more stress on the three-R's,"

"We should impose a strong censorship on the morality of books and movies," and "If you want a thing done right, do it yourself." We tell the student the nature of the topics, indicate what he is expected to do with them, and give him some hints of the sort of analysis that can be made. We give students an hour instead of a half hour to prepare and let them bring anything with them which might be of some use. One student came in with a dozen issues of *Time* magazine and did manage to find two telling references for his talk, but few are so fortunate. This problem of finding topics suitable for speeches also awaits a new solution.

DEVISING RATING FORMS

Papers can be read, and usually are, on the basis of a single letter grade; but there are so many intangibles, so many possibilities for a single factor to carry more weight with one rater than another, that it has seemed desirable to use a form that would require a uniform recognition of and a uniform weighting of certain qualities. We began with simple theme and speech rating forms and continue to use them, although they have undergone considerable modification. The first theme rating form had as its categories Point, Syntax, Grammar and Mechanics, Paragraphing and Organization, and Achievement of Point. Each of these categories was rated on a scale of 10 points, with 10 through 5 corresponding to letter grades A through F respectively. The Speech Rating Form was similar in format, but had as its categories Fluency, Physical Control, Vocal Control, Sense of Communication, and Point and Development of Point.

Before such a form is used the raters must know what they are rating in each area. To assure this, an "Explanation Sheet" was devised and, when raters did not use a category uniformly or consistently, the explanations were revised after discussion. For instance, a simplified description of "Point" read like this:

Does student narrow the subject down sufficiently? Does he make a point? (Narrowing a topic means matching the size of the subject to the length of the paper.)

The comment on "Grammar and Mechanics" appeared on the "Explanation Sheet" as:

These terms should refer merely to the decencies of literary expression, certainly not to Chinese puzzles of grammar nor to Handbook niceties that, commonly, no oriented person pays any attention to. Strict conformity to major grammatical correctness (avoidance of fragments, comma-splices and dangling participles) is essential. Beyond that, reasonable spelling, correct punctuation at major junctures, and the usual grammatical agreements answer the purpose.

THE WEIGHTING OF CATEGORIES

Beyond spelling out the content of each of the five categories in the Rating Form, there are further problems of the weights and the number of subdivisions in each of the five categories. We disagreed continuously on this matter. Should "Point" carry as much weight as "Achievement of Point"?

We have never been able to agree on the weighting of "Grammar and Mechanics." If we expect good mechanics before the student enters our course, should we give him any plus values for writing accurately? Should we not, rather, simply check these things if they are satisfactory and *subtract* points if they are not? Our disagreement here accounts for some of the discrepancies in our ratings, for two raters might well agree, in subsequent discussion, that a student wrote correctly though one had checked a 10 and the other a 6.

INCREASING THE RANGE OF SCORES

Another question is whether or not we can classify papers or speeches into ten different levels of goodness or badness on a given quality. Actually, we used only the upper six or seven numbers. This was due in part to the influence of those letter grades which were introduced above the numbers 10–5 and partly, possibly, to the time-honored association of 7 (70) with pass and failure.

To get as much spread between top and bottom as we could, we eliminated the letter grades over the numbers and wrote "superior" over the 10–9 and "unsatisfactory" over the 2–1, and pointed out that an average grade would be a 6–5. In this way we increased slightly the spread on the theme. Our total range on the theme, originally something like 47–22, was now more like 47–14.

LACK OF DISCRIMINATION IN RATING

Even when two raters did agree closely in total score they did not always agree for the same reasons. Such discrepancies suggested that, in some cases, the rating form was used only as a recording device for a grade previously determined by the rater. If, in his opinion, it was a C paper, then a series of checks down the 6 and 5 columns would take care of that! We were never able to eliminate completely this reading of a paper on the basis of a single overall impression with no discrimination of what quality was most or least influential in creating that impression.

Two studies were made to see if we could find out what distinctions raters actually did make when they were rating a theme and to see whether or not they marked one point independently of others. In the first, the staff rated several papers on the basis of about every possible point that a paper could be rated on—paragraphing, organization, content, spelling, punctuation, etc. There were over twenty-five categories. A statistical analysis of the results seemed to show that only one of these categories moved independently of the others. That was, as one might have anticipated, spelling.

Starring made a more detailed study.[1] He took 100 papers written for the Spring 1949 examination and weakened 20 of them in mechanics, 20 in sentence structure, 20 in diction, 20 in organization, and 20 in content.[2] He had these weakened versions copied in examination booklets in a handwriting similar to the original and had them graded with papers written specifically for examination purposes. He had the original ratings of these papers for purposes of comparison. He then had the staff rate these papers.

This study showed two things: 1) that at best the raters were distinguishing only three characteristics of a paper—something which we might call style, the choice of words, and the development of the idea, including both form and substance; 2) that raters tend to get an overall impression of the value of a paper and mark the rating sheet to agree with that impression. In other words, the weakness of a paper in mechanics suggests that it is barely satisfactory. So one checks the lowest score in that area and gives low average grades in the other areas in order to insure that the paper will receive a below-average grade.

SPEECH RATING

Since the Speech Rating Form also had five categories and ten possible points for each category, it involved some of the same problems. The five categories of the original form were 1) Fluency, 2) Physical Control, 3) Vocal Control, 4) Sense of Communication, and 5) Point and Development of Point. Here, clearly, we had eliminated the discussion of the weighting of "Point" by lumping it with "Development" (an organization-content heading). But this gave rise to another issue, particularly for those staff members who were not speech trained: shouldn't this aspect count more than 10 of the 50 possible points? After several years of discussion, "Organization" and "Content" became two areas on the form and thus counted 20 of the 50 points.

Possibly it was easier to win agreement on this point because of the presence of "Physical Control" on the original form. This category led to heated and violent discussion. "Should I give a man 10 points just because he walks up to the front of the room and stands there?" We agreed to put "Physical" and "Vocal Control" together, thus making possible the change recorded in the previous paragraph without increasing the total number of points possible.

"Fluency" as a category satisfied us, but we had to spell it out carefully in the light of our experience. It included grammar, sentence structure, word choice, silent and vocalized hesitations, repetitions, and reconstructions of thought.

The category "Sense of Communications" probably accounted to a great extent for the differences in our ratings, even though we readily agreed on what went into it. Here is one explanation:

Generally, this category refers to the speaker's awareness of the audience, subject, and occasion.

A sense of communication exists when the speaker gives a lively meaning to the words as he utters them.

The speaker should implement his communication by meaningful eye contact, direct questions, rhetorical questions, and polarized words, such as "I," "you" and "we."

The speaker should show evidence of enthusiasm and mental alertness; he should speak "with the audience" rather that "at the audience."

The speaker's composite performance should be considered in this category.

The last sentence invited a single, overall judgment of the speech. Certainly some of the details listed in this explanation consider things that raters probably checked elsewhere. Eye contact and gestures which help make "meaning lively" might well have been checked under "Physical Control." The way words are uttered is a matter of "Vocal Control." "Awareness of audience, subject, and occasion" cannot be completely dis-associated from "Organization" and "Content."

In any case, we revised the Theme Rating Form in the light of Starring's study. Since it seemed that we were rating for three things only, we reduced our categories to Content and Organization, Diction, and Sentence Structure and Mechanics. We then applied this same thinking to the speaking situation and came up with Content and Organization, Language, and Delivery. These later forms we have had to use only with the special permission students.

So far we have discussed the effect of the choice of topic on performance, and the construction and consistent use of a rating form. Both of these factors, plus at least one other—rater reliability—are involved in the final grades which result.

What exactly was our rating like? As already indicated, our speech rating has tended to be higher than our theme rating. This is also true of our day-to-day rating of speeches in class. We have hazarded two guesses as to the reasons. One is that the teacher, in trying to isolate the various qualities of a brief speech, misses something and cannot hear the speech again to identify a weakness he may have no notes on. So he gives the student the benefit of the doubt. The second possibility is that students are more competent in the spoken language than in the written one. They have used the one constantly and the other only intermittently. The reactions of our colleagues tend to confirm this; they rarely complain to us about students' lack of ability to speak. But perhaps they never give them a chance.

How well do we agree on speech rating? To rate speeches we assign three raters to a room and base the student's grade on the ratings of the two nearer raters if they are less than a grade point apart. If there is no agreement, we do give the student the average of the three ratings. Our experience indicates that with just two raters in a room, the worst pairing would give us a little less than 50 per cent agreement; the best about 70 per cent. With three raters we have quite consistently attained agreement between two raters 95 per cent of the time. Perhaps the mean of all three ratings would be a more reliable rating statistically, but it is less satisfying to the staff.

In spite of this high agreement between the two nearer raters we were not satisfied with the speech rating. For one thing, the smaller spread of the speech grades means that a smaller shift in total rating would change a student's rank in the group. Then when added to the theme and objective examination score, the speech score, lacking the extremes of the other two, seldom made a significant contribution to the final grade. Furthermore, the correlation of the speech grades special permission students received in the Fall 1956 examinations with their average class grades in speech is only .28, suggesting some lack of correspondence between the two.

RATER RELIABILITY ON THEMES

A look at the raw scores in theme rating is disquieting. A look at the average rating of individual raters is no less so. When raters read anywhere from 60 to 120 papers representing a slice of the student population based on an alphabetical arrangement of papers, they ought to have a fairly representative sampling of the papers. But frequently one rater would turn in his batch of 60 to

TABLE 24

GRADES GIVEN TO THE STUDENT ESSAYS BY 47 RATERS *

Paper	A	B	C	D	F
1	0	1	17	13	8
2	0	1	28	11	7
3	1	6	33	5	2
4	1	2	30	8	5
5	2	10	32	3	0
6	5	14	24	3	1
7	0	9	15	3	3
8	2	9	19	13	3
9	1	1	9	15	21
10	1	3	20	14	6

* Not all papers were read by all raters.

120 papers with an average of slightly better than B, while another returned his more-or-less equivalent batch with an average of D!

To investigate this problem, we selected a set of ten papers which were marked in common by 47 members of the staff. The distributions of grades given these ten papers appear in Table 24.

In the face of such differences in standards it would seem more desirable to have raters simply rank papers. This would eliminate at least the surface differences introduced by the fact that one rater is "hard" and the other "easy." The decision about what any given paper is worth would be postponed until the performance of the whole group was known. If the assignment was not quite fair or did not elicit typical student performance, we could make allowances for this in assigning grades. As yet we have not undertaken this system.

Part 2—Studies of Objective Test Items

ORAL RESPONSE AND ANALYSES

To gain some insights into the kinds of reasoning evoked by test items when responded to by students of varying levels of ability, four members of the Board of Examiners arranged at the beginning of one spring quarter to obtain recorded interview data from ninety-nine students who took final comprehensive examinations in Basic courses at the end of the previous winter quarter at Michigan State. The sample included about the same proportion of A, B, C, D, and F students as normally occurs in the whole population. Each interviewee had taken at least two comprehensive examinations at the close of the winter quarter which had just ended.

The data were obtained by interviewing each of the ninety-nine students in the sample, with one hour allotted to each interview. The interviewer asked each student to verbalize his thinking in arriving at the solution of 10–15 selected test items drawn from the examinations taken at the close of the previous winter quarter. During the interview the examiner had before him the original responses to the items given by the student several weeks earlier. The interviewer noted particularly the consistency with which the interviewee selected the *same* response again. When the student chose a different response than he had previously selected the interviewer asked, "Why?" "Are you sure?" or "How did you arrive at that answer?" Sometimes the interviewer asked, "Why did you change your mind? On the day that you took the comprehensive examination you selected No. — as the answer."

The data indicate that the students who earned A grades on the examination tended to be most consistent in selecting the right answers in both instances. This, of course, is to be expected. The D–F group, as would also be expected, showed the least consistency in selecting the right answer on both the examination and interview. The clean-cut distinctions sought between different categories of students simply do not exist.

One characteristic of students did stand out, however—that the lower ability level group did not read as well or as precisely as the higher level group. Another observation which confirms the expected was that the low scoring students were able to answer an item correctly with nearly the same frequency as the high scoring students when the item dealt with memorized factual information, particularly if the item happened to be stated as it originally appeared in his textbook or lecture notes. Items which involved somewhat elaborate comparisons not discussed in class, or which involved selection of certain outcomes and logical supporting reasons tended to baffle the lower ranking students more than the higher caliber individuals.

Our experiences in this project lead us to conclude that many of our most carefully constructed questions are apparently lost on our students. Some of the students are reluctant to engage in intensive prolonged thought on any question. In part this might be blamed on the artificiality of the interview situation, but to a greater extent it seemed associated with either a reluctance or inability to think, or a feeling that an item to which some answer was not immediately "obvious" was unfair. We conclude that the better an objective examination is the less likely it is to be cherished by the majority of our students.

VARIANTS OF THE MULTIPLE-CHOICE TEST ITEM

The wasteful character of the traditional five response multiple-choice test item has aroused an interest in exploring possibilities whereby such items can be made to yield more incisive results. When the student's performance on a traditional five response multiple-choice item is scored on a right-wrong basis, there is no indication of how far wrong the student was. There has been some experimentation with the weighting of wrong responses, but the results seemed unpromising. In the usual scoring procedure the student who eliminates three wrong responses, thus deciding that the correct answer is one of the remaining two, gets no better score than does the student who could not eliminate any of the incorrect responses. One can argue that this may be corrected by the operation of chance over the entire test. Yet one wonders if some method of scoring could be devised that would take into account the qualitative difference in these two students' abilities. Would not a system of partial credit serve to distinguish between the student who has partial knowledge and the student who has no knowledge in relation to a particular test item?

Dressel and Schmid [3] designed a variation in scoring the best answer type of multiple-choice item to make meaningful distinctions in the ability of students which are not disclosed by the usual all-or-none method of scoring the items. While their study was designed primarily to study the degree of certitude of student answers in three ability categories, the concomitant data it yielded on the functioning of test items proved to be equally interesting. The directions for the first variation, designated as the Free Choice Test, informed the students that while each item had but one best answer they should mark as many choices as needed in order to be sure that they had not omitted the correct answer. The directions also indicated that marking as few answers as possible would be advantageous, inasmuch as a correction factor to take account of wrong answers would be applied in scoring. Thus a student had the option of marking any likely answers— knowing, however, that credit gained for marking the right answer would be diminished by the number of incorrect answers he selected in the process. The scoring formula used was four times the number of correctly marked answers minus the number of incorrect answers, yielding nine possible scores for each item. The directions and method of scoring appear to take into account the student's certainty of knowledge about his answers.

Another variation, developed by the same authors and designated as the Degree of Certainty Test, directed the student to indicate how certain he was of the single answer he selected as the correct one by using the certainty scale: 1) positive; 2) fairly certain; 3) rational guess; and 4) no defensible basis for choice. The scoring system used made it possible to incorporate "certainty of choice" with the achievement score. This form of test measures certainty of choice more directly than does the free-choice form described above, but the procedure is much too cumbersome for use in large scale testing.

Another variation, the Multiple-Answer Test, informed the student that each item might have any number of correct answers and that his score would consist of the number of correctly selected answers minus the number of marked incorrect answers. This type of item forces the student to examine and weigh more thoroughly all of the alternatives, and thereby utilizes the potentialities of the item more completely than if only one answer is to be marked as correct. For reasons which should be apparent, some of us have called this the "multiple-confusion" item.

Analysis of performance data indicates that the free-choice item seems to differentiate the good student from the average and the poor student, but failed to distinguish sharply between the average and poor student. The degree-of-certainty item, on the other hand, differentiates all three levels of students about equally well.

Bakan [4] utilized the same free-choice item technique in a controlled experiment involving 540 cases. Her study brought to light no new data as to item functioning but substantiated the Dressel-Schmid finding that the failure of students to take full advantage of the free-choice item, as indicated by the disparity between actual range and potential or theoretical score range, may be due to long-continued, deep-seated conditioning to the marking of only one answer per item to which the students have been subjected in and prior to their Basic College test taking experiences.

Nelson and Schmid [5] explored another variation of the effectiveness of multiple-choice test items by using them in conjunction with the Angell-Troyer Self-Scorer. Degree of certainty of answers is revealed automatically by a built-in characteristic of this device—that the student is required to continue working on each item until he succeeds in finding the correct answer.

In the ordinary classroom test the student usually must wait a day or a week before he finds out which items on the test he answered correctly and which ones he missed. The student would benefit from an immediate knowledge of test results. Moreover, if he doesn't know the answer to a question the student should be most receptive of this knowledge at the time he is taking the test.

Pilot runs with the self-scorer at Michigan State suggested two hypotheses:

1. A test involving use of the self-scorer yields a wider score range than when the same test is used with standard answer sheets.

2. Use of the self-scorer increases test reliability.

For most students the jolt of having missed on the first try usually proves sufficient to prevent careless reading or naive selection of plausible distractors on the second attempt. Should the student miss on the second punch also, he usually makes a very thorough re-study of the item before punching again. In this respect, the self-scorer yields a more precise measurement because it not only reveals the student's ignorance but gives some indication also of the extent of his confusion. The self-scorer thereby maximizes the effectiveness of each test item.

If the student must go back and reconsider every item that he missed, he is confronted with a virtually new item after he has eliminated the wrong answer from further consideration. Obviously this lengthens the test. Since reliability is usually conditioned by test length, the second hypothesis listed above suggested itself. To test this hypothesis, a 60-item biological science test was administered at the end of the course to 110 students who recorded their answers on the self-scorer. Simultaneously another group of 125 students took the same test but this group marked their answers on standard IBM answer sheets. The former group completed an average of 35.6 items in a fifty-minute period, while the latter group averaged 40.1 items in the same length of time. Using as a basis for computing reliability only the first 30 items of the test for both groups, the Guttman L_4 reliability value for the self-scorer group turned out to be .95, while that for the IBM answer sheet group was computed to be .86. These results suggest that a non-speeded test will yield a higher reliability if the students record their answers on the self-scorer than if they mark their answers on standard answer sheets. Increased reliability in this instance stems from the more intensive use of each test item, which has the effect of increasing the length of the test.

Summary

Resistance to new ideas in examinations usually comes from the relatively inexperienced or from those who have settled into a comfortable routine which enables them to teach the course as an incidental activity while devoting major attention to other work. Examiners and examination committees must and do learn to live with the continuing dissatisfaction of this minority without entirely yielding to it. The real blocks to innovations in the examination lie elsewhere.

Practical difficulties stand in the way of some types of innovations in an examination which is taken by 4,000 to 5,000 students. Some of our studies have indicated, for example, that it would be desirable to expand the score range by instructing students to mark as many answer spaces as necessary to insure inclusion of the right answer. In a system which requires that grades be reported within 36 hours after the examination, the additional complications in scoring and processing rule out the change. Such a change would, as we know from reactions of students and faculty to the research activity on this problem, meet with other difficulties. Some faculty members reject the idea of credit for partial knowledge as encouraging shoddy learning habits. Some students not only find difficulty in adjusting to new directions of the type suggested, but actually react strongly and bitterly against such a change.

Flexibility developed by facing up to a wide variety of problem situations and repeated experiences requiring the student to demonstrate precise information and confidence in its accuracy must precede innovations in examination techniques which place a premium on such flexibility and certainty. An examination for all students in a course cannot overreach the content, the objectives, and the experiences which are common to all the sections of the course.

The preceding paragraphs of this summary apply primarily to the objective final examinations. There are present among the Basic College faculty—and this includes most of the examiners—those who, ideally, would like to see some use of essay materials in the final examinations. The difficulties of the Communication Skills staff in arriving at a satisfactory solution to the problem of obtaining and reliably reading essay material has not encouraged other departments to emulate them. As enrollment in courses increases from 3,000 to 4,000 to 5,000 and possibly higher, the possibility of using essay questions in final examinations for Basic courses becomes only an ingredient for a first class nightmare. Furthermore, the use of essay tests or any other experience in writing becomes less and less common within any of the courses other than Communication Skills.

What the course does not require the student to do, the final examination cannot reasonably require. Improvements in examinations take place slowly for they must go hand in hand with improvements in instruction.

Notes

[1] Robert W. Starring, "A Study of Ratings of Comprehensive Examination Themes When Certain Elements Are Weakened," unpublished doctoral dissertation, Michigan State College, 1952.

[2] These five categories were those appearing on the current rating form.

[3] Paul L. Dressel and John Schmid, "Some Modifications of the Multiple-Choice Item," *Educational & Psychological Measurement,* Winter 1953, pp. 574–595.

[4] Rita Bakan, "The Use of a Modified Multiple Choice Item Under Various Conditions," accepted for publication in the *Journal of Educational Research.*

[5] Clarence H. Nelson and John Schmid, "Some Characteristics of the SRA Self-Scorer," *Papers of the Michigan Academy of Science, Arts and Letters,* Vol. XXXVII, 1951.

At the End—Grades!

Grade Issues

Prevalent grading practice requires a condensation of the many and diverse efforts of students into a single symbolic letter. The summary judgment thus reported to registrar, student, and parents inevitably means different things to different people. Grades have been a recurring issue in the Basic College. There have been numerous subjective studies, and a few planned studies on the meaning, significance, and bases of the grades. This chapter is a summary of our deliberations and study and a delineation of present practices.

RAISON D'ETRE

Grades serve a variety of functions. The meaning and relative importance of those functions vary for instructors, students, parents, and college administrative officers.

Grades are used to:

1. Distinguish between students who receive credit for a course and those who do not.

2. Distinguish levels of performance among those who receive credit.

3. Summarize for the official record the student's enrollment and achievement in the course.

4. Inform the student of his achievement in a course.

5. Inform parents as to the progress of their sons or daughters.

6. Maintain scholastic standards by the elimination of the lazy or inept.

7. Motivate students through concern about low marks and satisfaction with the high ones.

8. Discipline students who fail to attend class or otherwise fulfill the contract implied by enrollment.

The first and third of these functions—credit determination and records—have encouraged the use of a single letter or number. An official record must be economical in form, so elaborate procedures are usually impracticable. In addition, the importance attached to granting credit practically enforces a composite judgment, on a fail-pass distinction, of all aspects of a student's performance. In a large institution operating on the quarter system the limited contact of an instructor with his many students makes anything more than a single and "simple" letter grade difficult if not impossible.

THE QUALITIES OF THE GRADE—THE IDEAL

A grade should possess a reasonable degree of objectivity, reliability, uniformity, and validity. The extent to which such characteristics are attainable varies considerably with courses and course objectives. Grading in a beginning mathematics course and grading in a studio art course are not identical problems.

Objectivity implies a grade based upon tangible evidence of achievement in regard to well-defined course objectives. This evidence should be carefully weighed according to principles sufficiently explicit and clear that other instructors seeing the same evidence and accepting the same principles would arrive at the same conclusion.

A grade is *reliable* to the extent that the student would tend to receive the same grade in another and independent grading. Sources of unreliability are found in the variability of the student's performance, in errors associated with the measurement techniques, and in the inconsistency of the individual instructor's appraisal of student performance. High student motivation, good evaluation techniques, and continuous effort on the part of an instructor to bring greater objectivity into the grading process are all conducive to increased reliability.

Uniformity in grading is an extension of reliability, referring to agreement among instructors as to the grade merited by the work of a particular student. This characteristic is relatively unimportant in single section courses, but in required courses involving several teachers it is essential that a student have some assurance that a given quality of work will be similarly appraised in all sections.

Validity requires that a grade be truly indicative of the achievement for which it is supposedly given. Two students with identical grades never have identical attainment, so the grade is at most a valid indicator of average achievement relative to all the objectives of the course. Usually, however, the grade will be an index of the average achievement with respect to some limited set of course objectives, perhaps those involving intellectual achievement. Lack of validity may result from failure to decide what goes into the grade, from procedures which measure only a portion of those outcomes upon which the grade is said to be based, or from unreliability in tests and judgments of performance.

The concepts of normality and symmetry, so often used in discussions of grades and grade distributions, are really irrelevant to the discussion of the qualities of the grade, although they may be appropriately used in describing grade distributions. The normal distribution—in the statistical sense of a specific mathematical distribution function—provides no basis for determining the percentages of various grades to be assigned, since the normal distribution of test scores can be divided at any desired points so as to yield any desired percentages of A's, B's, etc. The recurring contention, often confused with normality, that the percentage of A's and F's should be equal and that the percentage of B's and D's should be equal is more nearly implied by the word *sym-*

metrical. When there has been extensive selection, as there inevitably has been at the higher levels of education, the contention that a grade distribution should be either normal or symmetrical is a dubious one.

A WITCH'S BREW—THE PRACTICE

In studying the problems of grading, instructors were asked just what they utilized in deciding on a grade. Our purpose was to determine the extent of agreement or disagreement as to the basic elements upon which a grade is based. However, the factors that enter into a grade are partly conscious and partly subconscious. At the conscious level, differences exist among instructors over such issues as whether a grade shall be based upon achievement or improvement, whether it shall be based heavily on tests or primarily on day-to-day work in the class, and whether it should be based on attendance and attitude or solely on the demonstrated knowledge and intellectual abilities of the student. These issues are primarily matters of preference or point of view, although they may be codified by faculty action or administrative fiat.

The instructor who bases his grade to any considerable extent on improvement from the beginning to the end of his course encourages students to underperform in the beginning in order to show a marked improvement. The instructor who is influenced by apparent student effort may find himself the victim of "apple polishers." Lowering grades because of absence and making the grade depend upon the "attitude" of a student introduce into the grade elements irrelevant to the student's attainment of the commonly accepted goals of a course. Nevertheless, teachers admit to unsystematically incorporating such elements into a grade.

Many different factors are consciously or unconsciously incorporated into a grade and the significance of the factors often shifts from one student to another, but most teachers do strive for fairness and objectivity in the grading process.

Taking Things Literally

ALPHABETIC ALGEBRA

The final grade received in any quarter of a Basic College course is a composite of a grade given by the instructor and a grade obtained on a common final examination. Aside from a recommended distribution,[1] the instructors' grading practices are subject only to those strictures agreed upon by the entire department, such as a common midterm examination. In Communication Skills, the common final objective examination does not cover speaking or writing ability, so it is understood that the instructor's grades will be based primarily upon these two abilities. There is also an all-university policy that the instructor should take "due cognizance" of absences in assigning his grades.

Recognizing and accepting that the grades given by instructors are subject to variations resulting from differences in personalities, in standards, in emphasis on various aspects of the course or objectives, and a host of other factors, our system calls for offsetting these differences by the use of a common final examination. In practice it has been objective in nature. Good objective examinations avoid some of the sources of errors we have noted in connection with the instructor grade, but they have errors of their own. It is difficult to make an examination which gives due attention to all of the important outcomes of the course and which makes allowance for the reasonable differences in emphases of various teachers. By such averaging of an instructor and an examination grade we hope to minimize the errors.

'TWAS NOT ALWAYS SO

A great deal of thought was given to grading when the Basic College was first organized. In a program of required core courses a degree of uniformity in grading and in the treatment and the coverage of materials in classes seemed necessary. The quality and content of examinations not only reflects but influences what is done in the classroom, so good, uniform examinations were considered necessary. It was desired also that the examination require the integration of materials presented in the three quarters of the course. Finally, it was the intention to permit selected students to take the examination and receive credit for the course without having attended class. To achieve these purposes, it was decided that there should be a comprehensive examination covering all three terms of each Basic course. The student's grade on this comprehensive became his grade for the entire course.

The original intent was that there be no formal grading by instructors or that there be at most an indication of passing or failing at the close of the first two terms of the Basic courses. The insistence of the registrar that the lack of grades of the usual type would complicate or eliminate some of the statistical compilations; the concern of some of the personnel staff that decisions about continuation of scholarships, initiation into fraternities, sororities, athletic eligibility, and the like would be complicated by the lack of a grade at the end of each term; and the insistence of many of the instructors that such a grade was necessary for motivation of students—all of these factors resulted in the adoption of a policy of temporary grades issued by the instructor at the end of each term of a Basic course, with the ultimate elimination and replacement of these by the comprehensive examination grade.

Not more than a few months passed before many teachers were attacking the system on the grounds that it derogated the instructor to an inferior tutorial position. They argued that students tended to put off their work because they knew the instructor really had no great power over them. Part of the dissatisfaction certainly stemmed also from the lack of experience with the system. Shortly, the registrar and others who had at first been satisfied with the temporary term grade found that the re-computing of grade averages after the comprehensive examination was a major and highly fallible operation. Finally, students and their parents found it difficult to understand how an occasional individual who received satisfactory grades from his instructor over three terms could suddenly have all of these grades thrown out by failure on the final comprehensive examination.

Only the imperturbability of the dean kept the system in effect. His point of view was that the system should be given adequate trial and that this was not possible until it had been in effect over a considerable period of time. At his suggestion some surveys of student opinion regarding the examination and grading program were made, with the general result indicating a predominantly favorable attitude on the part of the students. But the opposition, both student and faculty, was highly verbal, and with a change in administration it was an expected and immediate result that a new system of grading was introduced. While many individuals regretted seeing the old comprehensive program abandoned, it would be unfair to say that anything was really lost in the process. On the whole, the purposes which had given rise to a single examination covering a whole year of work had never been achieved in practice. Indeed, short of eliminating from the staff individuals who would not accept the comprehensive examination ideal, the program could not be effective. The change was one of those practical necessities imposed by that combination of perpetual haranguing by dissidents, lack of backbone in proponents, and indifference by others which so often combine to defeat new and possibly significant educational adventures.

THE CURRENT GROUND RULES

The new program has already been partially described. In it the instructor gives the student a grade on a numerical scale, running from 15 to 1. This may be regarded as adding to each of the five letter grades (A through F) a plus and a minus. The examination is likewise assigned a numerical grade on the 15 to 1 scale. These two numerical scales are then added and letter grades are assigned to the composite on the following basis: 26 to 30, A; 20 to 25, B; 14 to 19, C; 8 to 13, D; and 2 to 7, F. To provide the instructor with additional control over students he may give a Y grade if approved by his department head. This eliminates the student from the final examination and gives him a failure. Students with failing grades must repeat the course in class. A student with a passing grade may retake the examination the following quarter; then he receives whatever grade he makes on the examination.[2] This system satisfies most of the criticisms leveled at the old, mainly because it is not markedly different in operation from practices in other courses.

An attempt has been made to maintain a cumulative quality in the successive term-end examinations, with the requirement being imposed that 10 to 15 per cent of the items should involve materials from the earlier terms of the course. We have discussed but have not as yet studied the extent to which this cumulative quality affects either students or teachers. We do know that many students object to it.

Studies of Grades

The studies briefly reported in this section by no means include all of the many ventures undertaken in trying to understand more fully the problem of grading. In certain cases the studies were undertaken in response to a specific question or a specific complaint on the part of a few individuals. In some cases the study of some aspect of the grading problem grew out of a question not directly involving grading. The first study that we shall discuss is an example of one of these.

THE "A STUDENT" MYTH

In the following chapter there is a discussion of the acceleration practices followed in the Basic College and a report of a number of studies of acceleration. Those antagonistic to acceleration felt that through acceleration the "A students" were soon eliminated from a course, so that in the second and third terms of a Basic course the quality of the class decreased and apathy increased.

We commonly speak in an offhand manner about "A students" and "B students" as though they were a more-or-less definite and permanent group. In the Basic courses which offer a continuing program from one quarter to another, a student might reasonably be expected to perform in a fairly consistent fashion from quarter to quarter. However, the situation is complicated by two facts: 1) we already know that many of the "A students" pass the comprehensive early and therefore do not continue in the course; 2) "F students" usually do not continue, and many other students, particularly among the low ability group withdraw from school. Yet the grade distribution, that is, the percentage of A's, B's, etc., remains about the same in succeeding terms of the Basic courses.

We decided, therefore, to take all students finishing the second term of Basic courses, look up their grade in the first term, and then determine what percentage of those making a particular grade at the end of the first term made the same and various alternative grades the second term. This analysis was done completely in the fall of 1947 and the winter of 1948 and verified on a sampling basis at several later periods. Only minor differences were found from one course to another and one time to another. Of all the students making A's at the end of the first quarter, 33 per cent made A's, 48 per cent made B's and the rest made lower grades at the end of the second quarter. Only 1.6 per cent of the students completing both the first and the second terms of the Basics received A's in both terms. It was estimated that of the entire group of students completing all three terms of the Basic College sequence courses only about one-half of one per cent make A's for all three quarters of any single course. Thus, of 3,000 students completing all three terms of a course, only about 15 students would receive A's in all three terms. In our own experience at Michigan State only 10 students out of 50,000 have made an all A record during their two years in the Basic College.

There is always the question as to how widely applicable are the results of educational research. It is doubtful that these results would apply in smaller institutions where the student might have the same instructor for two or even three terms of the sequence course with a resulting carry-over in grading. In our situation it is an exception for the student to have the same instructor. It is probably also the exception for the instructor to ascertain the grade made by a student in the preceding terms of the course.

HIGH STANDARDS AT "OTHER" INSTITUTIONS

One of the recurring complaints of college teachers is that their students are less capable than those of former years. This concern about decreasing ability and lower standards is not solely a local one and the faculty reaction is not entirely nostalgic.

General education courses—particularly those required at the freshman level—are particularly subject to criticism in the matter of standards. To some people it seems that any course which crosses departmental lines and is required of all students can be only superficial, lacking in rigor and standards of achievement. Our Basic College program faced and still faces comment of this sort, reinforced by the assumed fact that other similar institutions which have not introduced such programs have much more rigorous standards of achievement and grading in their freshman and sophomore courses.

One can readily accept that there are variations in standards from institution to institution, but the contention that the higher standards are enforced by "stiffer" grade distributions is less obvious. To discover whether the failing rate for freshman and sophomore courses is higher at other state institutions than at Michigan State, it was decided to try to collect some evidence on the distribution of freshman and sophomore marks at a number of midwestern universities. Although twenty institutions were asked for information on their grade distribution, usable results were obtained from only five universities. For five state universities, including Michigan State, the percentage of A's given to freshmen ranged from 10 to 15 per cent. The percentage of B's given ranged from 26 to 32, the percentage of C's from 37 to 44, the percentage of D's from 8 to 13, and the percentage of F's from 3 to 9. The distribution of sophomore grades tended to be slightly more liberal, and the distribution of marks for all under-graduates showed rather amazing liberality in some cases.

More surprising was the information from three of the state universities which operate under a policy requiring admission of all high school graduates. One might expect that the failure rate would be appreciably higher than in an institution such as our own which requires standing in the upper half of the high school graduating class in order to be admitted. The reported data exhibited no distinguishable difference. At Michigan State itself the grade distribution in freshman and sophomore courses out-side the Basic College was more generous in A's and B's than in the Basic courses. After these comparisons we felt that, if possible, the grade distribution should be based on clearly defined per-formance standards, and it was generally agreed that some liberalization of our grading distributions was in order. There seems to be no direct correspondence between institutional or professional standards and grade distributions. The standards of an institution are probably more influenced by admission policies than by any other factor.

DISAGREEING ON "STANDARDS"

The fact that the comparison discussed indicated that, if any-thing, we should give more A's and B's than had been the case renewed interest in the matter of whether standards of perform-ance could be agreed upon. An earlier study involved the use of final comprehensive examinations in one of the Basic courses. All instructors were asked to indicate the minimum passing score on this examination. The results were amazingly varied. This venture led to no usable conclusions, but it did not completely convince us of the futility of the approach.

A further investigation was resolved upon. The term-end ex-aminations of a particular quarter were chosen as the means of checking the agreement of instructors as to what standards corresponded to what letter grade. The task set with regard to examinations was to decide for each item whether it would be answered only by A students, by A and B students, by A, B, and C students, and so on. Our thought was that agreement among instructors might be more readily ascertained by requesting judgments about the difficulty of specific items on an examination than requesting a decision as to the score appropriate for award of various letter grades.

Instructors from six of the then seven departments of the Basic College cooperated in the task. The results varied from department to department, but it was clear that there was a great variation in the judgment of the difficulty of items. Most of the disagreement, however, was concentrated in judging those items thought to discriminate between the A and B and the D and F students. The amount of disagreement was greatly reduced when the usual five-category classification of A, B, C, D, and F involved in the instructions was reduced to three: above C, C, and below C. We felt that with sufficient time it would be possible to reach an *a priori* consensus on above average, average, and below average test performance. However, the achievement of such agreement would be possible only on the term-end examinations and it presented a task decidedly unattractive to the instructors. Furthermore, the approach held no possibility of achievement of similar uniformity for the instructors' term-end grades. Indeed, the achievement of such uniformity on the instructors' term-end grades was deemed unacceptable to the majority of the instructional staff.

The individual teacher preferred the utmost of freedom in determining his basis and standards of grading for the 50 per cent of the grade under his control. The examination performed its function best if the distribution of grades assigned on it approximated the overall distribution of instructor grades, thus preventing wholesale increase or decrease of student grades as they move from the instructor to the examination but still adjusting for some of the more marked discrepancies.

At one stage we returned to the idea that there should be a relationship between grading standards, at least at the pass-fail level, and admission practices. The thought was that we should not admit a student to a course if he were doomed to failure in it regardless of the effort that he put forth. There were many dissenters to the idea, particularly among those who felt that certain courses of the freshman year should perform a weeding out function, but we decided to investigate this possibility.

Immediately we found ourselves up against the problem of determining just what we meant by "effort." Most teachers indicated that they could tell what the student actually had accomplished but not how hard he had applied himself. The one tangible approach was to refer to residence hall reports to locate those students who were reported as not working. The assumption on which this approach was based was that students of low ability reported as not working should usually receive D's and F's in Basic courses. If not, and if the residence hall report on this point had any validity, it would seem that the average level of achievement was set too low. One study was made on this point in the spring of 1951, but that the rating on effort which was supplied from the residence halls was too informal and unreliable to have much meaning.

In further studies it was found that there was no meaningful relationship between residence hall reports on the work or lack of work by students and the grades achieved in the Basic courses. A more exacting study was undertaken in the fall of 1952.[3] The study involved obtaining reports from residence halls, from instructors, the Counseling Center, from the Improvement Services, and from the students themselves as to the effort made. The general hypothesis was that, among a group of students of low-level ability, effort or application should be a significant factor differentiating those who passed from those who failed. Again the results failed to support this hypothesis, either with regard to instructor, examination, or final grades. It became clear that even the lowest ability students do have the opportunity to make satisfactory grades, for even B's were occasionally found among this group, but what seemed to us to be the more obvious and overt aspects of effort or application were unrelated to achievement as appraised by instructors or by examinations.

SEX AND/OR PERSONALITY

One of the more startling results of one investigation was that in the restricted sense of acquiring grades personality can be a reasonably good substitute for sex. The investigation— a doctoral study by Kelly [4]—which resulted in this finding was initiated in an attempt to explain why some individuals consistently received higher grades from their instructors than they received on the common final examination, while others reversed that pattern. Kelly's first selection of the extremes exhibiting these two patterns led to a simple explanation. With only one or two exceptions the group with consistently higher instructor grades was composed of females. Women consistently get better grades from the instructors than they do on the examinations, while the men reverse the situation though to a lesser degree.

When the sex differential was adjusted out by selecting separately men and women with consistent and sizeable bias in favor of either instructor or examination grades, another pattern emerged. The high instructor grade group was largely composed of students of inferior ability, who were highly motivated in the direction of placating authority figures by prompt fulfillment of each and every assignment. They appeared to depend heavily on memory and, either because of inability to reorganize their knowledge to deal with novel test situations or because of sheer inability to read and grasp the tasks presented, they found difficulty with our examinations. The high examination grade group, in contrast, was largely composed of high ability students who had confidence in their own powers and were disinclined to complete assignments in which they saw no value. Many of this group in the interviews held with them were highly critical of the Basic courses, avowing that they found no challenge in them.

Sex and personality apparently do play a role in obtaining grades. Even more important, however, is the implication that personality factors should be more carefully studied to determine whether there may be any meaning for instruction. We hope to explore this lead further.

RATIONALIZING WITH STATISTICS

We have accumulated two types of statistical data which give us some confidence that our dual method of arriving at a grade has some merit. The first of these involves the correlation between instructor and examination grades. Obviously perfect or near perfect correlation would indicate that the two approaches simply duplicate each other while very low correlations would raise serious questions as to validity of one or both methods of grading. Correlations were found to vary with courses but to be consistent from term to term and year to year. In Natural Science and in Social Science the correlations of examination and instructor grades were found to be consistently in the range of .55 to .70. The results in the Humanities course were slightly lower. For Communication Skills, in which it will be recalled that the instructor and the examination grades are directed to different objectives, the correlations were lowest. These latter ranged from .35 to .55. These results seemed to us to accord with common sense.

The second type of statistical evidence pertained to the percentage of correct answers corresponding to various examination grades. Lacking absolute standards, we should still like some assurance that the same performance would receive the same grade. We know that student groups taking a particular part of a Basic course do vary in ability from term to term. Since we prepare new examinations each term we have no assurance other than the competency of the examiners that successive examina-

tions are equivalent in difficulty. We take some satisfaction, however, in the fact that term after term we have required a
minimum of 70 to 80 per cent correct responses by students in
order to receive an A. The student earning a minimum C has to
answer correctly 45 to 50 per cent of the questions. Minimum
passing grades require correct response on 35 to 40 per cent of
the items. These ranges, applicable generally over all four courses,
can be further narrowed if achievement standards are stated for
individual courses.

Those individuals addicted to thinking of an A as ranging
from 93 to 100 per cent and a minimum passing grade as 70 per
cent are shocked by such data. It should be kept in mind, however, that we consciously strive for examinations of such difficulty
that the average score will be about 50 to 55 per cent of the
questions. This is desirable in order to achieve a maximum range
of scores for discrimination among grades. We do not delude ourselves into believing that passing students really master 70 per
cent or more of the material covered in our courses. In any case,
whether our performance standards for the various grades are
good or not, we take some comfort from the evidence that we
have achieved some degree of consistency in holding to them.

A Point of View About Grades

The basic difficulty in relating grades to standards is that
grades cannot be used to enforce standards which are not defined
in terms meaningful to both instructors and students. When
clearly defined goals are lacking, grades and examinations, whatever their source, become potent elements in defining the objectives of a course because they are the most tangible expression of
them. To take the position, however, that examinations and the
grades derived from them entirely determine the amount and the
kind of work that students do is to take an unduly pessimistic
view of human nature. The monthly paycheck is the most obvious
reward of the teacher, but no teacher worthy of the name consciously attempts to equate his efforts to that check. Many of the

real rewards of teaching are to be found elsewhere than in the financial returns. Learning must have some of the same motivations, and part of the teacher's responsibility is to arouse them.

Both the abiding values of a general education and the more significant immediate ones depend on the affective as well as the cognitive characteristics of individuals. The habits, attitudes, beliefs, assumptions, interests, and values of an individual coupled with his intelligence will, in the long run, determine the quality of his contribution to society much more than will the knowledge or even the methodological techniques he learns in college. These affective qualities are not readily graded in an objective manner, and any attempt to grade them must be regarded with some suspicion as verging on an authoritarianism not consistent with the freedom of opinion and action permitted the individual in a democracy. If the view is accepted that many (and perhaps most) significant outcomes of education are not subject to grading, the students should be so informed. The grade in a course should be defined as based upon knowledge and upon those intellectual skills for which correctness and accepted standards provide the possibility of reasonably consistent evaluation for all individuals. Finally, the grading on this basis should be handled in the most expeditious and inconspicuous fashion possible, with the teacher assuming the obligation of emphasizing other ungraded outcomes and working out means whereby students may evaluate their own progress toward these goals. Such a conception implies a rather different attitude toward examinations, grading, and student-teacher relations than is commonly found in the classroom. It is unlikely that such a state of mind will ever be achieved throughout a large staff and student body.

We are convinced, therefore, that there is no solution of the grading problem entirely satisfactory to all concerned. Students would like all A's, administrators would like few F's, and the teachers would like to be left alone. Grading is inevitable and we must continue to strive toward making it less inaccurate, but always with the awareness that overemphasis on grading is not conducive to good instruction. Admission that grades in the formal sense cannot and should not encompass all the desired outcomes of education is a necessary requisite to so defining and determining them that a degree of objectivity and uniformity can be introduced. Then, *perhaps* the grade can be relegated to its proper place as an irritating and incidental, though necessary, element in the educational process. At the moment at which this is written, we seem to have made some progress toward this goal.

Notes

[1] A's, 0–15%; B's, 20–30%; C's, 40–50%; D's, 10–20%; F's, 0–10%.

[2] In recent years only about 60 students per year have taken advantage of this provision. On the average, 38 of the 60 received a higher grade, 19 the same grade, and 5 a lower grade.

[3] Leonard S. Laws, "A Comparative Study of Basic College Grades and Effort-Interest-Attitude Ratings for Low-Ability Students," doctoral dissertation, Michigan State College, 1953.

[4] Eldon Kelly, "The Study of the Discrepancies Between Instructor Grades and Term-End Examination Grades Among Basic College Students at Michigan State University," unpublished doctoral dissertation, Michigan State University, 1956.

10

LEWIS B. MAYHEW and
WILLARD G. WARRINGTON

On the Credit Side

Credit by Examination

The faculty of the Basic College realized from the beginning that some entering college students had already had extensive experience in the fields covered by its courses in general education. Service in the armed forces, home environments, or attendance at an outstanding high school might have given students such advantages that the Basic courses would be repetitive. Economy of staff and student time suggested that these students not be required to take the courses. For these students, the issue was not really acceleration but simply recognition of accomplishment and proper placement.

Other students, lacking in specific experiences relevant to the Basic courses, still possessed such superior general academic aptitude that they could do the same amount of work done by average students in much less time and indeed might find no personal challenge unless they were urged to do so. For these students, the issue was the need for providing for differential rates of progress which may fairly be called acceleration. The program in the Basic College, by which students may acquire academic credit by passing an examination, is designed for both of these classes of students.

THE RATIONALE FOR CREDIT BY EXAMINATION

At Michigan State a total of forty-five quarter hours of gen-

154

eral education credit is required of all students who matriculate in the University. A required sequence of courses for all students is inconsistent with what is known about individual differences, and is without special provisions for students deficient in essential skills and for the very capable or the more mature student. Michigan State maintains an elaborate series of remedial or improvement services to help students develop basic skills in reading, speaking, writing, and arithmetic. This provision for students lacking facility in those skills is paralleled by the provision allowing students to complete work early by taking examinations.

We are not unaware that remedial work is very expensive and that the credit by examination feature actually saves money. In fairness to the able student and to ourselves, additional inspiration and challenge must be provided for these individuals. Plans for such a program are under development. By providing for the special needs of the top and bottom of the student body, the objection that the Basic College curriculum is too rigid is met. Furthermore, class and teacher time is gained for those students in the middle range of abilities who comprise the bulk of the college population.

HISTORY OF CREDIT BY EXAMINATION

Michigan State has long had the policy that any student may gain credit for any course in the catalogue by examination. To do this he must obtain permission of the department offering the course, and this permission must be validated by the student's own dean and the dean of the college granting the credit. The registrar grants the official statement of permission.

In practice, this policy has not been widely implemented in the upper schools and colleges of the University. Less than 0.2 per cent of the students in the period 1949–50 received academic credit by examination in courses outside the Basic College. There have been a few notable instances, such as one student earning 149 quarter hours by this means and another 65 quarter hours. Most of this 0.2 per cent, however, was made up of students gaining credit in relatively few courses, such as physical education, typing, and shorthand. Many of those acquiring credit were seniors who, lacking three or four credits for graduation, sought out some course—any course—in which they might acquire easy credit. Our study of this has led to some tightening of the practice of giving permission for taking examinations for advanced credit in order to eliminate what might be considered abuses.

The Basic College differs from the other colleges by making acceleration through examinations an integral part of its total educational program. Students have been offered the option of remaining in Basic courses or seeking credit by taking an examination before registering in the course. Those considered qualified by the department concerned take the same examination as taken by students registered in the course. If they successfully pass this, full academic credit is awarded and recorded on their transcript of credit.

Although there is some variation from department to department, the usual practice is for all students to enroll in the first term of a three-term Basic course. The student doing A level work at the mid-point in that first term may be granted permission to take the examinations in the second and third terms of the course. A student enrolled in the second term of the course, with his final grade from the first term and his mid-point grade in the second term making a B-A pattern, may receive permission to take the third term examination. If these students earn an A or a B on the examination (a C for students 28 years of age or older), they are given credit with the grade earned on the examination. Failure to perform at the prescribed level results in no grade and the requirement that the student enroll in the appropriate term of the course.

CHANGING PRACTICES

Substantially this system has been in effect since the initiation of the Basic College in 1944. However, as the college has changed there have been alterations in the examination program as well. When students were being evaluated in the Basics by a comprehensive examination over the entire course, students given permission at any point in the course to take the examination early took the complete comprehensive examination. Such students had to cover a full year's work in preparation for the examination. Now, in place of the single comprehensive examination, students are required to take a common term-end examination after each term of the course. Students accelerating are thus required to study only the specific term's work for which they are granted permission. Under this new system, the accelerating students at first were not required to take the examination for the term of the course in which they were enrolled; rather, they received the instructor's grade. Administrative problems of scheduling require that the three term-end examinations of each Basic course be held on a single day, and three two and one-half hour Basic examinations on the same day are impossible to arrange as well as inhuman. We now require the student to take all examinations. The administrative problem is met by asking students taking two examinations for credit to postpone one for a quarter.

DECREASING USE

The examination-credit program of the Basic College has proven successful in some respects but has not achieved its prescribed purposes in others. Each year approximately 4.5 per cent of the total credits earned in the Basic College are earned through examinations alone. Most of these are earned by students accelerating in only one term of one Basic course, although there have been a substantial number of students accelerating in several to all four courses. There has, however, been a slight tendency downward in the proportion of credits earned by examination during recent years.

Part of this decrease can be accounted for by changing the

level required to receive credit from a C to a B. Part can be explained by a gradual restriction of the policy for acceleration. Each one of the changes in the system has made acceleration seem undesirable for more and more students. The shift from the comprehensive examination to term-end examinations was accompanied by a shift in emphasis in the examination proper. Comprehensive examinations, covering a full year's work, relied on many questions involving applications of principles rather than sheer recall of information. The term-end examinations, by emphasizing specific content of a course, made it more difficult for students to capitalize on broad related background experiences. The most recent change forces students to postpone for one term at least one examination. Since such postponement might, if the attempt proved unsuccessful, dislocate their program of courses, it is anticipated that some students will prefer the safer way of continuing in the course.

The proportion of students seeking credit by examination has varied markedly from department to department. In the seven-course curriculum students received permission much more frequently in the courses Written and Spoken English, Effective Living, Biological Science, and Social Science than they did in Physical Science, Literature and Fine Arts, and History of Civilization. In part, these differences resulted from more restrictive permission policies in the latter departments. The nature of certain examinations also discouraged students. The examination in Physical Science, for example, emphasized specific knowledge taught in the course. The attitudes of the students toward a course also accounts for some of the differences. Thus students saw Written and Spoken English and Effective Living as repetitive of earlier experiences. History of Civilization, however, they saw as a new experience for which it was worth remaining in the course. Similar differences hold true under the present four-course system. The Humanities Department grants about one-third as many permissions as the other departments and, of that number, a smaller percentage succeed in gaining credit.

Fears and Facts

HOW CAN THEY POSSIBLY PASS?

When the comprehensive examination system was planned, those responsible believed that students taking the three terms of a Basic course would perform better on examinations than would students given special permission. For this reason they decided that grades should be determined by the range of examination scores earned by the regularly enrolled students. From the first this belief was not substantiated, for it simultaneously led to careful screening of those permitted to take the examination. Thus, the special permission students markedly out-performed regular students. Indeed, it was difficult to decide on a grade distribution fair to those enrolled in the course which would not yield A's and B's for the entire examination-credit group.

When this phenomenon became known, many persons next theorized that these students, being relatively more able, were earning their grades by high scores on the portion of the examination covering the work they had taken in the course, with their performance on the rest of the examination based largely on some general ability to reason. Careful analysis of a number of examination subscores refuted this hypothesis. Special permission students, regardless of the course, performed about equally well on questions for each part of the course. (This finding should be qualified by noting that since the change from the comprehensive examination system to the quarter system there has been one department in which special permission students have regularly performed less effectively than regular students on all examination questions except those which require the interrelating of material from several portions of the course. On this one type, the special permission students have out-performed regular students.)

The fact that students who have not had the course could out-perform students who had taken the course led to a different sort of criticism. The argument was that the examination must be an intelligence test rather than measure of what was taught in the course. The pre-test data reported by Jackson in Chapter VII and the careful study of the examinations demonstrated conclusively that this criticism was unwarranted. Furthermore, the shift to the term examination has tended to increase the factual emphasis of the examination, since each one is based on a smaller segment of the course.

WHY DO THEY ACCELERATE?

One important reason for the establishment of the special permission feature was to allow students to speed up their academic careers. With the veteran population after World War II, this purpose was realized. Veterans, feeling the press of time and age more keenly than the usual undergraduate, earned about eleven quarter hours of Basic course credit by examination as compared with five credits for non-veterans. Many veterans saved a full term's work or more. Some students still see acceleration as a means of cutting down financial outlay by shortening a college course but, on the whole, the students now in college do not reduce the college period by acceleration. Even those students who accelerate in several Basic courses do not graduate any earlier; nor do they give earlier graduation as a reason for wanting to accelerate. Most accelerates want to spend more time on their major or on other elective courses. Quite a few want to accelerate so as to have a lighter schedule in their junior and senior years. Some simply feel that they have unusually good backgrounds and should take advantage of the opportunity to accelerate. The faculty of the Basic College has recognized all of these reasons as appropriate to a program of acceleration but the majority favor an enriched educational experience.

Of significance in judging this entire matter of motivation are the reasons why qualified students do not accelerate. They become interested and want to finish the course. Especially was this true of History of Civilization under the seven-course system. Many just did not feel competent to pass the examination without taking the course. Others did not wish to risk getting a C or B when an A might be insured by taking the course. Still others do not accelerate because they lack time to study for the examination, and a few are concerned that credit earned by an examination may not transfer to other institutions. This latter concern is justified by experience, and is most curious and not a little irritating. Credit by examination is not a rare practice and very frequently no distinction is made on the transcript between credit by examination and credit by regular enrollment in the course. When the distinction is made, a few institutions refuse to recognize such credit.

When the comprehensive examination system was changed to a series of term-end examinations, students granted special permission were not required to take the examination for the term in which they were currently enrolled. Typically, the grade they received at the mid-point of the term from their instructor became their final grade in the course. Considerable faculty suspicion was generated that students were applying for special permission only to safeguard a high grade earned at the mid-term. They felt that students were not making any effort to study on the assumption that they might be lucky and pass the examination. In one study, 19 per cent of the special permission students admitted to this motivation in seeking permission. All term-end examinations are now required.

DO THEY PREPARE?

Of even more concern to the faculty was the possibility that students were not studying adequately in preparation for the examination. There is a fairly widespread belief that academic achievement should signify a certain minimum amount of work, and that students who do not expend this effort are undeserving of academic credit. Actually, students receiving special permission put in considerable time in study in relation to the total time available to them after being formally granted permission. The formal approval of requests for special permission is typically issued about a week and a half before the end of the term. The median study time for students in one course is between 20–25 hours and in another course between 11–15 hours. In the first course, 14 per cent of the students who actually gained credit by examination studied over thirty hours, and in the second course, 10 per cent studied over forty hours. These figures suggest that students spend about half the time on preparation for the examination that enrolled students normally spend in class. How they use the time will, of course, vary markedly from student to student. Those who are successful seem typically to make as honest and as conscientious an effort to prepare for it as time allows.

Characteristics of Those Acquiring Credit by Examination

What differences exist between students who do take advantage of the special permission provision and those who do not? What differences exist between those who succeed and those who fail to acquire credit after permission has been received? We have partial answers to these questions.

Students accelerating are generally more able than those who remain in the Basic courses. Their academic aptitude is higher, and their reading ability better. Of these two factors, reading ability is most important. This is consistent with a common-sense consideration of the problems students encounter in gaining credit by examination in the Basic courses. Each course demands a great deal of reading. In the Social Science course, for example, each term's work requires an average of seventeen full pages of reading every class day if students are to complete the course requirements. Since the term-end examination is based on the textbooks in the course, ability to read these materials adequately in a relatively short time is a prerequisite for success. It also follows that students who accelerate in several Basic courses have better reading ability than those who accelerate in fewer Basic courses.

In addition to reading ability, there appear to be some personality differences between successful accelerates and students who do not receive special permission. Both groups were tested with an *Inventory of Beliefs* which purports to divide students along an authoritarian-non-authoritarian continuum. On the authoritarian end, individuals seem to be rigid, conforming, dogmatic, anxious, and uncomfortable. They find it difficult to shift mental sets required for varying types of problems. They are addicted to stereotyped thinking and are highly ego-centered human beings. At the other end of the scale are persons who are relaxed and comfortable and find it unnecessary to be on the defensive. They can deal with abstract materials, and can suspend judgments for considerable time without suffering undue anxiety.

Students who accelerate tend significantly to come out at this latter end of the scale on the attitudes test. This is consistent with what we believe to be the nature of the task confronting accelerating students. The orthodox way of college study is to read a text, go to class, listen to lectures and take notes, and then write an examination. The instructor assumes a great deal of the responsibility for course organization, which the authoritarian person likes. To do these things independent of an instructor requires considerable flexibility and self-direction on the part of students. An examination covering unknown materials can be viewed as a threat or as an opportunity. Instead of reacting with panic, the non-authoritarian person responds by searching for rational ways of overcoming the problem. From the evidence available, the rational approach is just what the successful accelerate employs.

The attitudinal or emotional differences seem not to be related to students' participation in extra-curricular activities. It was theorized, for example, that students who accelerated were likely demonstrating a kind of aggressiveness which would also be demonstrated in active campus life. There appear to be no differences with respect to participation in extra-curricular activities between accelerating and non-accelerating students, even when their abilities are held consistent. Non-accelerating students actually tend to join fraternities and sororities more often than the special permission group. Perhaps the accelerate is primarily concerned with more academic-related matters.

Students who gain credit by examination earn higher all-university grade point averages than do students who remain in the Basic courses. However, within this phenomenon lies a curious factor. Students who accelerate at every possible chance do not make any higher grade point averages than students who are eligible but do not take special permission. The most able students apparently exercise some discretion in which Basic courses they try to "write off." This, when considered with the very deep concern some students have for grades, suggests a picture of students keeping an eye open for where their best chances lie— a not unreasonable approach.

Some faculty members have feared that students who gained credit by examination in Basic courses would be inadequately prepared for relevant courses in the upper schools of the University. To determine whether or not this fear was warranted, two groups of students were compared with respect to the grades earned in certain upper school courses. Each group had performed well enough in their Basic courses to have entitled them to special permission. One group took advantage of the privilege while the other did not. Although the samples were quite small, no differences in upper school achievement between the groups were detected. In another inquiry comparing accelerates to non-accelerates, the special permision group actually performed better in related upper school courses than did those who remained in the Basic course for the full time.

Summary

The system of special permission to gain credit by examination has proven a feasible undertaking for a large complicated university. It is accepted by faculty and student body alike as an essential feature of the Basic College. Even those students who reacted against basing their entire course grade on one comprehensive examination liked the special permission feature of the comprehensive system. Students are quite aware of the possibilities of the system, and some students study very hard to gain permission to accelerate. These able students are thus allowed to spend more time on their major studies or to broaden their education or to enjoy leisure.

The system has prevented what might otherwise have become a rigid system of required basic education by providing a way for between 4 and 5 per cent of the students to gain exemption from one or several terms of Basic courses. Students have been perceptive in the ways they took advantage of this possibility. They tend to seek exemption from those courses which they feel duplicate work they have already had and to remain in courses they find interesting. Since students are also realists, they tend to seek exemption where they believe they have the best chances for success and high grades. They steer away from examinations which are, by reputation at least, difficult.

Although the system has gained the support of the majority of the Basic College faculty, there are misgivings about certain aspects of the program. Many faculty members still are suspicious that an examination cannot appraise the values they see emerging from classroom work. They feel that students who gain credit by examination cannot possibly be as well qualified as those who gain credit through class attendance. Evidence to support or disprove such fears is very difficult to obtain, for the values involved are not well defined. The tendency has been toward restrictive policies for implementing the program. Whether in the long run these tendencies will result in elimination of acceleration will depend on a number of different factors.

It is significant that the Basic College program gained its acceptance at the time when the World War II veteran population entered colleges and universities. As that source of students dried up and the much smaller school population born during the depression years entered college, various restrictions were placed on students seeking to gain credit by examination. In view of the large numbers of students soon to reach college age, it can be predicted that interest in effective acceleration will again mount.

Whether this will result in an intensification of the examination technique or in some other device will be determined in part by what other measures are taken to challenge able students. Many faculty members feel that they would like to meet the individual needs of these students through formal programs of curricular enrichment rather than formal programs of acceleration. Some of the able students apparently share this view. The relative merits of these two approaches need to be explored so as to make clear the conditions under which each might be appropriate.

Part IV

THE
PERSONNEL
TOUCH

11

JOHN W. KIDD

The Students Live

The Residence Hall in Education

An institution can ill-afford to regard college controlled housing as simply a matter of providing food and a roof. Whether or not it is planned, it is true that the students who spend many hours of their day in college and university residence halls will experience certain influences on their habits and points of view as well as on their skills in interpersonal relations.

The rapid growth of Michigan State University and the relatively small size of the community in which it is located have necessitated a very rapid development of housing facilities for students. Such a state of flux is not conducive to careful study of the attendant problems. Nevertheless, there has been an attempt throughout the period of growth to provide in the residence halls the kind of staff and student supervisory and guidance personnel which would make residence hall living a significant educational experience.

The studies to be developed in this chapter happen to have been made in the men's residence halls, and were carried out in a somewhat formal way largely because the individuals involved happened to be ones trained in educational research procedures. As an aside, it is in itself a commentary on the unintegrated nature of higher education that men's and women's residence halls tend to be handled in separate offices and with a minimum of coordination. Considering the fact that only since World War II have colleges and universities regarded marriage as a respectable state for students it is perhaps not surprising that segregation of the sexes in the residence halls and in the administrative offices concerned with residence halls continues to be the rule in the vast majority of institutions of higher education.

A wide acquaintance with principles and practices in the operation of residence halls on college and university campuses reveals that many types of programs exist varying from the extreme of simply providing a shelter for students to incorporating the residence hall into the planned educational process.

The Residence Halls at Michigan State

STATEMENT OF PHILOSOPHY

The philosophy of residence hall operation at Michigan State has varied over the years with changes in administrative personnel, expansion of plant, and fiscal pressures. Research reported here was based on the rationale that ". . . the residence hall can be and should be a scene of guided growth and development for the individuals concerned; growth in the sense of achieving intellectual and social maturity of personality; development in the sense of achieving social as well as academic competency not likely to emerge from classroom experience alone." [1]

GENERAL EDUCATION

With the establishment of the Basic College in the mid-1940's, Michigan State began a program of general education for all students. This program continues to involve the requirement that approximately one-fourth of the credits needed for the baccalaureate degree be experiences common to all students, irrespective of major field. Just what these experiences should be has remained flexible as changing times and new evidence justify the inclusion and exclusion of certain items.

While this core of general education was and is most often conceived of as wholly academic, it seemed to many of those concerned and particularly to some of the residence hall personnel, that for those who lived in residence halls such living itself constituted part of an educational core. (It may not be amiss in this connection to consider the feasibility of requiring one year of such residence hall living of all students.)

EDUCATION OF THE WHOLE PERSON

A major tenet of American education is the idea of "education of the whole person." In that so much of this "whole person" is a product of informal as well as formal out-of-class activities and associations, it would seem logically sound that the institution attempt to guide these out-of-class learning experiences in much the same way that it guides in-class learning opportunities—toward desirable goals for the "whole person."

Continued consideration of such a possibility brings one to several conclusions:

1. the largest time block of out-of-class learning involves, for the typical boarding student, his place of residence;

2. if the institution is to seek to guide personality development in such a setting as the residence hall, it must be informed as to similarities and differences in the residence hall as compared with the classroom, insofar as they have implications for learning;

3. the financial and other aspects of residence hall operation in most institutions of higher education make the tutorial system, whatever its merits, impracticable;

4. sources of direction for individuals in residence halls are for the most part found within the peer groups of which they are a part;

5. only through an understanding of peer groups and their dynamics is the institution able to participate intelligently in residence hall educational guidance.

Residence Hall Research at Michigan State

It is, therefore, inevitable that the major goal of early research in the residence halls at Michigan State should be the increased understanding of group dynamics. This implies, among other objectives, an effort to understand the factors associated with different degrees of selection-isolation-rejection, and the factors associated with informal peer group leadership. Only with such information at hand could one reach rational decisions as to:

1. the propriety of either attempting to alter or modify group-leader structures or working through them toward acceptable educational goals;

2. the chances for success of a program designed to enhance the acceptability of isolated and rejected individuals;

3. the probable efficacy of programs of leader-training;

4. the desirability of imposing various categories of staff and/or student personnel on the residence hall in supervisory-consultative or guidance functions.

THE SOCIOMETRIC APPROACH

Sociometry, the measurement of interpersonal relations, is generally derived from the work of J. L. Moreno.[2] In essence sociometry is the utilization of individual responses to confidential questions, about selection and/or rejection of other individuals according to such criteria as friendship or leadership, to achieve a quantified measure of the relations of individuals to each other. As an example, each member of a group may be asked individually and confidentially to name the person(s) he would most prefer as a partner in business, or as a guest in his home, etc. A tabulation of responses will yield a measure of the acceptability of each individual by the others in such a role. Further, one may chart the structure of groups, sub-groups, and inter-group relations among the individuals questioned.

Other than observation, which involves varying degrees of reliability, there is no way of getting a true picture of the feelings of individuals about other individuals except as they are willing to state such feelings truthfully. Since the question of truthfulness—validity—of responses constantly plagues the studies of expressed attitudes, evidence of reliability and validity of the studies reported here will be cited.

THE LEADERSHIP PRINCIPLE IN GUIDANCE

Enough research has been done to reveal the significance of peer group leadership in the behavior of group members.[3] In light of such research, it was recognized that the influence of imposed functionaries, staff or student, in the residence hall might very well rest upon their acceptability to the concerned groups as real leaders and not merely nominal ones. This, in turn, led to speculation about methods of selecting persons who would have such status and the possibility of locating real leaders and giving them official status instead of the traditional method of conferring nominal status on selected individuals and hoping or assuming that they would achieve the role of real leaders.

To follow this line of investigation, it was necessary to know more about the types of individuals that were most frequently selected by residents of residence halls as their friends and leaders as well as the types most frequently rejected in these roles.

Evidence on Selection-Rejection

A study of the men in one residence hall was made in an attempt to discover traits consistently associated with highly rejected persons as opposed to their opposites, the highly selected persons.[4] The residence hall in question housed 639 men representing an unselected sample of all academic classes and categories of male college students.

Each individual was asked to complete a confidential questionnaire naming his best friends, those least liked, those he would prefer as leaders, and those least preferred. From composite scores of such selection and rejection, the highest 102 individuals were considered the "selects" (these had all received ten or more positive citations), and the 96 individuals with less than two positive citations were designated as "rejects."

The questionnaire also called for certain personal data, and additional facts were gathered from other sources.

Treating all frequencies by the Chi-square test of statistical significance, it was found that such rejects were different from selects at or beyond the 5 per cent level of confidence, in that the rejects more frequently than the selects:

1. were persons of atypical ethnic identification and/or foreign nationality.

2. were persons from communities of more than 100,000 population.

3. were persons of lower academic class.

4. were persons who interacted least with other group members.

5. achieved lower course marks (with ability factor held constant).

6. changed residence and dropped out of school.

7. were ignorant of family income.

8. rated themselves lower on scholastic effort.

9. rated themselves and were rated by their nominal leaders as lower on "Personality Adjustment."

In comparing even more extremely differentiated selects and rejects—the highest 21 and lowest 21 out of 639 students in the same group studied by Kidd and reported above—Mill[5] found that the rejects significantly more than the selects:

1. were characterized by unusual or eccentric thinking.

2. had less desirable "test-taking attitudes."

3. had less self-esteem.

4. showed psychopathic characteristics.

5. showed less willingness to accept responsibility.

6. showed maladjustment (though neither was a normally adjusted group).

7. suffered more anxiety.

8. held widely deviant percepts.

9. expressed hostility through devious measures.

10. were less frank and open in behavior.

Since the two studies involved the same persons, evidence of validity and reliability of sociometric choice is common. Ninety-four per cent of the residents returned the questionnaire on a voluntary basis. The questionnaire differentiated among individuals as to friendship and leadership status. All seriously rejected individuals who had come to the attention of the administration prior to taking the questionnaire were so identified by questionnaire returns.

The personal data called for by the questionnaire was subjected to a sample checked with outside sources where applicable (such as academic standing and age), and agreement was consistent.

Evidence on Leadership

In the study of leaders in men's residence halls, the characteristics most frequently desired in student functionaries by fellow students were: 1) friendly, cooperative, and pleasant; 2) responsible; 3) mature and respected; 4) intelligent and capable; 5) considerate; 6) moral; and 7) quiet. The characteristics least desired in their leaders were: 1) unfriendly; 2) carefree; 3) immature; 4) incapable; 5) inconsiderate; 6) immoral; 7) loud; 8) conceited; 9) deviant; and 10) unstable.[6]

These opinions were obtained by asking 525 male college students in one residence hall to name, on a confidential questionnaire, the fellow resident(s) they thought would be good officially designated leaders (Resident Assistants) and those they thought would not be successful in such a role and in each case to give reasons. A tabulation of these reasons (answers to "Why?" when a name was cited) resulted in the lists of characteristics reported above.

The evidence of validity and reliability of this study is impressive. Ratings by the incumbent student functionaries (Resident Assistants) of other leaders were consistently verified by the ratings of the general population. The 16 functionaries in office at the time (and who had been selected as a result of similar sociometric data) were rated among the highest 20 of the 525 students involved in leadership status.

Evidence—Then What?

In reference to rejection, Kidd [7] recommended that the institution concerned adopt the following program:

1. In the case of foreign students and others of markedly atypical ethnic type:
   a. attempt to bring them to a realization of the many differences likely to exist between their previous cultural values and the values of the culture in which they now find themselves;
   b. suggest that the mark of an educated man is adaptability—that they may make certain adjustments to these different values without forever forsaking their earlier values to which they may return;
   c. attempt to get across the idea that to really understand another individual and anticipate his actions and reactions, one must think as he thinks—therefore, adjustment to the values of a group and the individuals therein necessitates taking on the roles of various individuals within such a group;
   d. show that effective role-taking is essentially a communicative process, a matter of interpersonal relations of a sympathetic sort; that to effectively put oneself in another person's place one must at least temporarily abandon bias, prejudice, dogma, and *a priori* answers;
   f. arrange situations, programs, activities, and conditions insofar as feasible to increase the sheer quantity of contacts by atypical group members with the more typical ones.

In the case of other rejects, the institutional officials might call their attention to the kinds of behavior typical of most rejected and most selected persons, and how adjustment to norms of acceptable behavior in such a group constitutes a vital part of the educational process and is real preparation for successful living in the American society.

This does not call for conformity so much as the development of rationality, in that the only basis for behavior which will meet rational criteria is that behavior which exists in the society in which one operates. To be aware that one's behavior is conforming or non-conforming, that it is accepted as normal or not, is possible only in light of definitions representing the mores of others about one.

Those highly selected by their peers, on leadership criteria particularly, should be recruited (preferably indirectly) into the residence hall program as recognized (and possibly officially designated) student leaders.

The effectiveness of such "real" leaders being utilized as "designated" leaders is indicated by the reactions of one of the residence hall managers who admitted skepticism at the outset of the program but who, after some five years of relying on sociometric data for identification of leaders, said (in part): ". . . the quality of leadership attained by employing this system conscientiously will amaze even the most experienced college and university officers." [8]

Notes

[1] John W. Kidd, *Residence Hall Guidance* (Dubuque: Wm. C. Brown Co., 1956), p. 1.

[2] See particularly his *Who Shall Survive?* (Washington, D.C.: Nervous and Mental Disease Publishing Co., 1934).

[3] See as examples: Helen Hall Jennings, *Leadership and Isolation* (New York: Longmans, Green and Co., 1943); Leslie D. Zeleny, "Objective Selection of Group Leaders," *Sociology and Social Research,* March–April 1940, pp. 326–336.

[4] John W. Kidd, "An Analysis of Social Rejection in a College Men's Residence Hall," unpublished doctoral thesis, Michigan State College, 1951.

[5] Cyril R. Mill, "Personality Patterns of Sociometrically Selected and Sociometrically Rejected Male College Students," *Sociometry,* May 1953, pp. 151–167.

[6] John W. Kidd, "Positive and Negative Leadership Traits in a College

Men's Residence Hall," *The North Central Association Quarterly,* April 1955, pp. 360–362.

⁷ John W. Kidd, "An Analysis of Social Rejection in a College Men's Residence Hall," unpublished doctoral thesis, Michigan State College, 1951, pp. 158–161.

⁸ Charles H. Clark, in the Foreword of *Residence Hall Guidance,* by John W. Kidd (Dubuque: Wm. C. Brown Co., 1956).

12

ROSS W. MATTESON

And Counselors Learn

As indicated in Chapter 1, the programs of general education and counseling at Michigan State developed concurrently, and there has been increasing awareness among faculty, students, and administrators that counseling can be an integrating factor in general education. This view of the counselor's integrative role in general education is shared with Hardee and her collaborators in *Counseling and Guidance in General Education*.[1]

A program of general education, both in its objectives and in the opportunity for curricular exploration which it offers to students (and staff), is quite in harmony with the philosophy underlying the provision of counseling services. The counselor sees in general education a potentially ideal environment for helping the student to define and clarify his goals. But even the best of general education programs do not solve all of the problems of students. Indeed, certain aspects of general education may even increase the problems. Counselors can and do deal with the emotional problems frequently found in students confronted with general education requirements and materials. And in the area of academic achievement, counselors and Basic College instructors at Michigan State cooperate in developing special programs in reference to study habits, deficiencies and academic difficulties, referrals for remedial help, and special work with "gifted" students.

Although the Counseling Center at Michigan State is administratively a division of the Dean of Students' Office, many of its functions are tied in with the work of the Basic College. Ease of access and communication between counselors and Basic College administrative staff members has aided in serving their common interests in students.

Counselors occupy a strategic position for certain kinds of evaluative studies of concern to general education. We have been interested in two somewhat different but interrelated programs of study, one designed to help counselors in learning *about students* and the other to help counselors in learning more *about the counseling process.*

About Counseling

STUDENTS WITH PROBLEMS

Records of the Counseling Center over the past several years show that nearly 80 per cent of the student counseling contacts are with Basic College students. As shown by Warrington in Chapter 4, 42.6 per cent of entering freshmen made at least one visit to the Counseling Center during their two years in Basic College. The corresponding figure for transfer students was 26.9 per cent over the same period. Some students make only a single call at the Center; others may become involved in extensive counseling covering many interviews. An increase in the average number of contacts per individual student has been observed in the past few years.

Recognizing the impossibility of neatly categorizing the mixture of problems which students present, counselors have nevertheless attempted to make rough approximations of what they consider to be the content or area of each problem contact. Educational and vocational planning has been consistently the most frequenty checked category, accounting for from 30 to 40 per cent of all contacts. Academic problems and problems of personal-social adjustment have been next most prevalent. Approximately 10 per cent of the student counseling contacts are referred for additional help or information to other persons or services.

Weekly and quarterly summaries of data from contact cards and other records have enabled the Counseling Center's executive committee to "keep a finger on the pulse" of counseling activities and have served to facilitate advance planning. But certain significant questions with respect to contacts remained unanswered. Consequently, a sample survey [2] was designed to get at such issues as the interrelationships among types of contact data and the trends among repeat contacts.

Analysis of the coded data from a sample of 460 contact cards indicated that students visiting the Center represented the entire range of academic aptitude and, as with the majority of students, were likely to have expressed preferences or majors. Most of them were Basic College students seeking counseling on their own initiative. Although counselors assigned individual testing in a number of cases, the use of tests was not a routine procedure. Many of the students are one-time visitors seeking specific information or assistance which is supplied or which results in referral to some other office. A request for information on and interpretation of orientation tests brings a number of students to the Center each term.

Students who made more than just a few visits to the Center were likely to have been first-year students referred to the Center by others and to have been students of slightly below average academic ability, originally enrolled as "no preference." These students present problems of vocational planning, of academic difficulty, and of personal nature, which require more extended contact.

Judging from the sample of students studied, it appeared that contacts classified as "personal-social" were more likely than other types of contacts to have been referred to the Center by others. Similarly, as would be expected, these cases were the ones most likely to be referred on to the Mental Hygiene Clinic. Counselors tended to hold longer interview sessions when working with students whose problems fell in this category and the approach was more likely to emphasize the attitudinal and affective elements.

The trend of repeat contacts for these students was found to be toward a shift in problem area as counseling progressed. Shifts in counseling emphasis were also noted in a number of cases, with more of the shifts in the cognitive than the attitudinal direction. Many problems are too complex to be classified into meaningful discrete categories, while basic inadequacies and anxieties may find expression in first one and then another student "problem." Thus, as counselor and student work through the problem presented, there quite naturally will be a change in the manner of viewing the problem and in the approach employed.

SOME TOOLS AND TECHNIQUES

Prominent among counselor's tools and techniques are the various kinds of psychological tests and of course the counseling interview. Counselors have from time to time conducted studies aimed at the more effective use of existing measuring devices, as well as the development of new instruments. One general result of our work with tests has been an increased awareness and appreciation of the contribution that these instruments can make to the effective counseling of students. Coupled with this is the developing point of view that test results are not the complete nor the final answer; that test scores for an individual need to be interpreted with caution, and that consideration must be given to those variables which the tests do not measure.

Through a study of client participation in the test interpretation interview [3] it was found that those students who participated most actively did gain the most in self-understanding from the test interpretation interview. Client-to-client variation in the amount of participation elicited by an individual counselor, however, was not related to these self-understanding changes. It was the mean client participation index for clients of individual counselors which was significantly related to the mean gains in self-understanding made. The data from this client-participation study gave also some confirmation to the hypothesis that students who participate most are more secure in their vocational choices.

Such studies as this one contributed to the growing volume of knowledge about the technique of counseling and helped counselors to realize the importance of technique. As general education seeks to draw out the student, to expose him to new and vital experiences, and to present him with opportunities for growth through making decisions, so the counseling technique seeks to place more and more emphasis on the active role of the client in thinking through his problems and making his own plans.

PREDICTING ACADEMIC SUCCESS

Counselors are quite naturally concerned with the possibility of predicting college success. From time to time attempts have been made to check on the predictive effectiveness of such generally used tests as the *ACE Psychological Examination*. We have been especially interested in prediction studies of students admitted to college through such special programs as "testing and counseling for admission." Jackson has already discussed in Chapter 6 a study of our earlier procedures in admission by testing.

The individualized approach to college admission at Michigan State involves counseling as well as testing. Both pre-test and post-test interviews are included, the latter enabling counselor and candidate together to go over the test results. Scores are interpreted in such a way as to give an idea of the probability of success in college. Where indicated, the counselor may suggest alternative possibilities or, as sometimes happens, the applicant himself may want to discuss the advisability of a somewhat different type of training. We have found that the academic performance and survival in college of students admitted through testing and counseling appears to be somewhat better than that of students admitted under the earlier group entrance examination plan. Of even more value is the opportunity afforded by the testing and counseling procedure for these people to be inducted into a program of higher education under more or less ideal personalized conditions. Impressions, suggestions, and recommendations of counselors have come to be essential and often determining factors in the consideration of college applicants. This holds not only with respect to their actual admittance but also to the type of curriculum and credit load recommended for a beginning student in his first college term.

Farwell's [4] more recent evaluation of the "T & C" procedure tends further to support our program of individual testing and counseling for admission. His evidence emphasized the effectiveness of the counselors in gaining insights about college applicants which enabled them to make meaningful recommendations as to the admittance of "borderline" applicants.

Through continuous evaluation of student selection procedures, it is hoped that greater effectiveness can be attained in admitting to college those students who will profit most from a program of general education.

EVALUATING OUR EFFORTS

In education we are continually evaluating our efforts to ascertain the extent to which objectives are being attained. These evaluations are sometimes formal, sometimes informal.

One way of evaluating the impact of a college counseling center on students is to question them about it. Results of a study [5] seeking to measure student attitudes toward counseling by means of a *Counseling Attitude Scale* were favorable. The Counseling Center and the counselors were given a strong vote of confidence by approximately 84 per cent of the students sampled.

A number of the students questioned had never called at the Counseling Center at all and had apparently derived their positive attitudes toward the Center from the experiences of acquaintances. It was this thought, plus the observance that considerable segments of the student population did not seem to be aware of the Center's existence (or at least its function), that prompted a further investigation into students' perceptions of the Counseling Center.[6]

This study asked students to rate their attitudes on scaled continua concerning their freedom to bring certain types of problems to the Center for help. From an analysis of these ratings, it appeared that students felt freer to seek help at the Center for educational than for emotional problems. This perception appeared even stronger if they had attended one of the summer counseling clinics. Females felt freer than males, and lowerclassmen (boys and girls) felt freer than upperclassmen to seek academic advisement. Students who had made previous visits to the Center indicated much less reluctance to come in with educational problems than students who had never visited the Center. Something of a dichotomy was apparent in student's perceptions of the Center's services: there was a tendency for students to see the Center as an appropriate place to bring their social and personal problems or their educational and vocational problems, but not both.

One key phase of Counseling Center activity at Michigan State has been the program of summer clinics made available each year for incoming freshmen. These clinics are designed to help bridge the gap between high school and college by providing: 1) an orientation to campus life, 2) an appraisal of academic aptitudes and skills, and 3) the services of counselors to assist in college planning. The employment each summer of a number of regular Basic College instructors trained in counseling techniques has served immeasurably in enhancing the value of the clinic program.

Evaluative studies of the clinic program [7] have indicated that students who have attended the clinics consider the experience most helpful. Suggestions made by participants on the evaluation forms provided have led to numerous modifications and innovations in the program. As summarized by Goodrich:

In general, the counseling clinics have proved very popular and worthwhile. They have helped facilitate, for incoming freshmen, the transition from high school to college. They have enabled new students to develop greater self-understanding of their assets and liabilities. They have helped to eliminate some of the inevitable confusions and frustrations of freshman week that prevail at most educational institutions. While it would be naive to assume that orientation problems can be completely solved by clinics, such data as are available suggest that considerable progress has been made.[8]

About Students

In learning about counseling, counselors learn also about students. And conversely, in seeking to learn more about students, we are quite likely to gain insight into our own ways of behavior in dealing with students' problems. Some of the things which counselors at Michigan State have sought to learn about students have centered about their interests, their majors, their concepts of self, and their special problems.

THEIR INTERESTS

Growth in the breadth and intensity of students' interests and experiences is a commonly stated objective of general education. A series of Counseling Center studies have focused upon the relationships existing and the changes brought about in students' interests and experiences. In an initial attempt to investigate these relationships, the *Kuder Preference Record* was employed experimentally—with altered directions—both as an interest test and as an experience inventory.[9] Although it was found that in general a student's expressed interest in a certain area tended to be conditioned by the extent of his experience in that area, the approach used was considered not totally satisfactory. Accordingly, the problem of how interests become modified with experience—specifically the experience provided by a particular type of general education program—was again approached, using a somewhat different type of instrument.

A composite inventory was designed, composed of items within the experience range of students. The "Activity Check List," as the experimental inventory is known, provides for two-fold responses keyed to ten areas of experience-interest. It has now been given to several thousand students. Used with a group of nearly 700 entering freshmen [10] the inventory provided comparative expressions of interest in some of the academic and other college activities available to them. A desire for new experiences was especially apparent in such activity areas as personal-social relationships, the aesthetic, and the recreational. Another finding of significance was that the combination of high interest scores with low experience scores tended to be associated with low academic aptitude and low socio-economic level.

Another phase of the experience-interest studies has been concerned with longitudinal changes in students' interests in accordance with the broadened experience patterns available to them through participation in a program of general education. [11] In this case, students who had responded to the Activity Check List as entering freshmen repeated the same inventory at the close of their second year of college. Analysis of increases and of discrepancies in interests and experiences over the two-year period tended to confirm the hypothesis that students' interests do become modified in the course of their exposure to (and participation in) a program of general education. The expressed hope that the impact of two years of college should result in broadened interests for everyone is not a vain one, even though a minority of students do fail to register the hoped-for gains. Subject to acknowledged limitations—and anticipating the need of further analysis focused on patterns of responses—two broad suggestions have been advanced: [12]

1. Objectives dealing with the breadth and intensity of interests as educational outcomes probably merit continued study and consideration as attainable goals of the general education program.

2. It is possible that the counseling of students during their first two years of college may be made more realistic when the probable effect on interest patterns, at the time of entering college, of impending educational experiences is taken into consideration.

THEIR MAJORS

The interests of students ordinarily find expression, in part at least, in their choices of college majors. Mention has been made of the Counseling Center's role in assisting Basic College students to explore their interests, along with other significant factors related to the characteristics and requirements of college curricula and vocational objectives.

Some of the factors and problems present in connection with changes of college major have been studied from time to time in the Counseling Center and elsewhere. One early survey, concerned with the nature of the changes of major authorized by counselors, analyzed over 4,000 such changes.[13] As hypothesized, changes authorized during registration periods were less likely to be rated as "good choices" than those effected during the course of a term where adequate time for counseling could be made available. It was found that changes out of, or into, the "no-preference" category constituted one of the most significant— both in terms of numbers and in terms of counseling impact—of the changes authorized. A more extensive type of counseling appeared to have entered into those cases where students faced with the uncertainty of choice had elected to begin college with no preference and were able through counseling to come to a decision based on a consideration of pertinent factors involved. Counselor judgments as to the appropriateness of a student's major choice were found to be associated positively with the extent of counseling involved in the change, thus lending credence to the belief that choice of vocation and curriculum is a process rather than merely an event.

In a second phase of the series of preference change studies, over 600 of those students who had entered college without any definite majors were studied. Among findings for this group of "no-preference" students was the disclosure that about one-half of them had chosen a major within their first year of enrollment. Significantly, the major choices of the "no-preference" students, once selected, appeared to be more stable than those made by students who had indicated a preference upon first entering college.

A third preference change study investigated certain concomitants of curriculum preference changes.[14] Characteristics of the individuals making various kinds of changes were also studied. Data were collected for a total of over 1,000 students who had entered college at the same time and who had made one or more changes of preference during their two years in Basic College. A control group of 500 students who made no changes of major during this period was used for comparison. Findings of the study were organized around five major question areas, having to do with characteristics of students with various change patterns, characteristics of the changes themselves, results of the changes, relationships to academic performance, and the role of time in the selection of majors. Some of the more significant findings were:

1. Of all students making changes, those who had started as No-Preference enrollees and decided later on a definite major had entered college with the most favorable prognosis of success.

2. Most of the initial changes of preference occurred during the first year of college and most students made no more than this one change.

3. In general, changes of major preference tended to be accompanied by improvement in scholastic performance. Also, there were fewer dropouts during the first two years of college among the students making curriculum changes than there were among the non-changers of the control group.

Our work with individual students faced with the problem of choice, as supported by the evidence from these studies of preference change, has led to such recommendations as:

1. No stigma should be attached and no penalty should be assessed to students who choose to make changes of major preference while in Basic College. It appears desirable that students be permitted and (where indicated by counseling) even encouraged to make approved changes.
2. The performance of the "no preference" group in this study, plus the fact that relatively few students remain in "no preference" an undue length of time, gives further evidence that this manner of beginning college work holds much promise for certain categories of college freshmen.
3. It is apparent that students changing or contemplating a change from a major to "no preference" are particularly in need of continuous counseling and follow-up attention.[15]

THEIR "SELFS"

To learn about students is to be sensitive to their problems and characteristics as individuals. One of the most enlightening approaches to an understanding of students is the self-concept approach. Several aspects of this problem have recently been considered at Michigan State. One Counseling Center study utilized a self-evaluation scale to consider certain kinds of self-estimates of a group of 419 beginning Basic College students.[16] Focus was upon indexes of aspiration and of discrepancy as derived from the self-evaluation scale. Self-estimates of experience-interest relationships and the prediction of students' own college achievement were also considered.

In general it appears that students consciously approach the start of college with lofty goals and great expectations. This is a time when both counselors and instructors may utilize fundamental motivational factors. Furthermore, the early detection of unrealistic aspirations and objectives can be of strategic advantage in the counseling of these students.

In the matter of forecasting students' first term achievement, significant association was found between predicted and earned grades. While freshman women were less optimistic than freshman men in their grade predictions, they were also more likely to anticipate improvement within the two-year Basic College period.

As an extension of the study of self-estimates of college freshmen, certain aspects of student self-concepts have been considered in relation to counseling.[17] Design of this study provided for analyzing differences among counseled, non-counseled, and "one-stop" groups of students. The Self-Evaluation Scale revealed no very significant distinctions between students seeking and not seeking counseling, except perhaps in the matter of "interest aspiration." Here the counseled groups showed significantly higher mean aspiration indexes (prior to counseling) than did the non-counseled students. There was no evidence that counseling-seekers were prompted by the possession of any less self-understanding than their fellow students.

In spite of rather obvious limitations, there seem to be certain implications in such findings as mentioned. For one thing, significance of the interest factor for students seeking counseling points up the responsibility of counseling to capitalize fully and fairly on the characteristic eagerness, hope, and expectation of freshmen to extend their horizons of academic and vocational interests. On the other hand, we perhaps ought to give more attention to such issues as counseling's obligation to lead the individual toward developing realistic attitudes and goals, even at the expense of "lowering" his (unrealistic) aspiration level. It has been shown that improved self-understanding is an attainable goal of counseling. Probably significant progress in this direction can best be realized when self-understanding is sought and taught as a consciously recognized objective of counseling. In so doing, counseling makes a significant general education contribution.

THEIR PROBLEMS

When individuals seek counseling, what things are disturbing them? Earlier in this chapter reasons prompting individual students to come to the Counseling Center were summarized. At this point it seems appropriate to mention also a few of the special groups of students with more or less common types of problems with which counselors from time to time become involved.

Two "special group" studies, one dealing with superior or "gifted" students and the other with students on academic probation may be summarized by way of illustration. In studying the problems of the intellectually gifted freshman, a committee of counselors sought through individual interviews to learn something of the characteristics of these students and their reactions to the experience of college.[18] Although a certain pattern of background, attitudes, and desires characterized many of the superior students, the wide variation existing among these freshmen of high academic potential was impressive. The exploratory investigation has led to the conclusion that a variety of things, including individual attention for superior students, could be utilized to help them better to realize their full potential. In an earlier study of women honor students, DeLisle [19] reported a tendency for these women to possess a better than average degree of self-understanding.

In her case study of students on academic probation, undertaken at the request of the Basic College Dean, Fessenden [20] interviewed 65 students who failed to qualify academically for admission to an upper college at the end of the Basic College period, and analyzed confidential reports submitted by the counselors to whom most of these students had been referred for further individual assistance. Through this approach she was able to study the varying effects in different individuals of similar motivations, e.g., exceedingly strong desire for vocational preparation.

Such factors as limited academic aptitude, choice of major seemingly inappropriate to the individual's aptitudes, and personal-social-emotional concerns were also considered. This individualized approach to the study of academic deficiency revealed relationships which may be lost in the statistical study of large groups of students on probation. The findings lent support to the practice of allowing some students to use the Basic College period for exploration or for changing or modifying goals without being unduly penalized academically for initial immature judgments. They also point up the great need of many students in academic difficulty for counseling assistance—sometimes in lieu of instruction in academic skills.

Some other Counseling Center studies over the past few years that can only be listed have involved groups of: 1) applicants considered as "potential problem cases"; 2) students having excessive absences; 3) World War II veterans admitted to college through a special refresher program; 4) students with speech difficulties; and 5) students with reading disabilities.

About Research

Through Counseling Center research we have learned some things about students and some things about counseling. We have come to realize that individuals not only differ from each other but that an individual today is different in many ways from the same individual yesterday and tomorrow. Levels and patterns of interest, for example, change as new experiences become available. Insofar as these changes are reflected in students' college majors, the selection of an educational or a vocational objective becomes a developmental process. Temporary uncertainty and changes of major become less deadly sins.

In learning about counseling our efforts in connection with tests, with client participation, with individualized admissions, with summer clinic evaluation, have all served to emphasize the significance of the interacting roles of individual student and individual counselor.

The research studies that have been described in this chapter have been primarily of the type ordinarily considered as "action" research. We have been interested in finding answers to questions growing out of our work with students and applying to our counseling procedures. Since counseling and general education do have much in common—in the way of goals, opportunities, facilities, and methods—many of the implications of Counseling Center research may find adequate expression only in the total effort of the whole general education program.

Notes

[1] Melvene Draheim Hardee, Editor, *Counseling and Guidance in General Education* (New York: World Book Company, 1955).

[2] Ross W. Matteson, "A Survey of M.S.U. Counseling Contacts," unpublished manuscript, 1956.

[3] Paul L. Dressel and Ross W. Matteson, "The Effect of Client Participation in Test Interpretation," *Educational & Psychological Measurement,* Winter 1950, pp. 693–706.

[4] Gail F. Farwell, "A Coordinated Program of Admissions and Counseling," *The Personnel and Guidance Journal,* December 1956, pp. 236–240.

[5] Arnold L. Form, "Measurement of Student Attitudes Toward Counseling Services," *The Personnel and Guidance Journal,* October 1953, pp 84–87.

[6] Paul T. King, "Student Perceptions of the Counseling Center," unpublished manuscript, 1956.

[7] Thomas A. Goodrich, "Gains in Self-Understanding Through Pre-College Clinics," *The Personnel and Guidance Journal,* April 1953, pp. 433–438; Ross W. Matteson, "Counseling Clinics for High School Grads," *Occupations,* April 1951, pp. 502–505; Thomas A. Goodrich, "Precollege Counseling Clinics," *Minnesota Studies in Student Personnel Work: Counseling and the College Program,* Ralph F. Berdie, Editor, pp. 19–26.

[8] Thomas A. Goodrich, *op. cit.,* p. 26.

[9] Paul L. Dressel and Ross W. Matteson, "The Relationship Between Experience and Interest as Measured by the Kuder Preference Record," *Educational & Psychological Measurement,* Spring 1952, pp. 109–116.

[10] Ross W. Matteson, "Experience-Interest Relationships as Measured by an Activity Check List," *Journal of Counseling Psychology,* Spring 1955, pp. 13–16.

[11] Ross W. Matteson, "Experience-Interest Changes in Students," *Journal of Counseling Psychology,* Summer 1955, pp. 113–120.

[12] *Ibid.,* p. 119.

[13] Ross W. Matteson, "Changes in Curriculum Preference Made by Basic College Students," *College and University,* January 1951, pp. 257–264.

[14] Ross W. Matteson, "Concomitants of Changing Curriculum Preference," *College and University,* January 1953, pp. 223–235.

[15] *Ibid.,* p. 235.

[16] Ross W. Matteson, "Self-Estimates of College Freshmen," *The Personnel and Guidance Journal,* January 1956, pp. 280–284.

[17] Ross W. Matteson, unpublished manuscript, 1956.

[18] Frances H. DeLisle, Donald L. Grummon, and Dorothy R. Ross, "The Intellectually Gifted Freshman," *Basic College Quarterly,* Fall 1956, pp. 5–11.

[19] Frances H. DeLisle, "A Study of the Relationship of the Self Concept to Adjustment in a Selected Group of College Women," unpublished doctoral dissertation, Michigan State College, 1953.

[20] Beatrice I. Fessenden, "A Case Study Analysis of Factors Contributing to the Academic Deficiency of Selected Michigan State College Students on Probation," unpublished doctoral dissertation, Michigan State College, 1953.

Part V

THERE ARE
SOME CHANGES
MADE

13

PAUL L. DRESSEL

In Critical Thinking

The objectives stated for general education—as well as specialized education—invariably display some concern about cultiva-
tion of the ability to think. Yet there is little evidence that
consistent efforts are made to this end. The mental operations
implied by thinking are not well understood; the means for pro-
voking and cultivating thinking on the part of individuals are
not entirely clear; and the seeming necessity of covering large
masses of material in the classroom leaves too little time for any
but the most able students to reflect on the meaning, interrela-
tionship, and applicability of knowledge which is being gained.
The able student, too, often displays reluctance to think for himself, in part because the exercise of thought and judgment is
time-consuming and difficult and in part, no doubt, because he
sees little evidence that such effort will yield returns in the cur-
rency of the academic realm.

The various courses of the Basic College have consistently
given prominence to the development of thought and judgment
although the terminology chosen has varied. The Communications Skills staff has viewed critical thinking as the integrating
element underlying the communication skills. The Natural
Science staff has, from the beginning, attempted by selection of
material and by careful planning of laboratory experiences to
develop in the student understanding of and the ability to use,
the scientific method. Similarly the Social Science and the

Humanities faculties have viewed their task as that of acquaint-
ing the students with the ideas and concepts of their fields—not
just for the sake of knowing but in order that the individual student become better able to think through for himself the issues
which confront the human race generally, and our society in
particular. Quite naturally, then, attention to the objective of
critical thinking has received considerable attention in our
examinations and in our studies of changes in students.

Knowing and Thinking—A Pseudo-Conflict

Anyone who emphasizes the importance of providing opportunities for the student to think for himself runs the risk of being
accused of de-emphasizing the importance of knowledge. That
one cannot think productively about a problem without relevant
knowledge is self-evident. It is easy to argue from this that the
initial courses in an area should concentrate on adding to the
store of knowledge and that only at some later date should significant thinking be expected or even permitted. The fallacies in
such reasoning are many and obvious. The encyclopedic mind
is not necessarily a thoughtful one. Thinking depends on knowledge, but is not automatically triggered by weighty accumulation of facts.

Knowledge, other than simple observed facts, results from
thought and cannot be acquired on other than a rote basis except as the individual engages in a thought process which
extracts the essence and relates it to previously acquired knowledge. To argue that one cannot think until he has acquired
relevant information is to ignore the fact that recognition of
relevancy is in itself a thinking process. It is significant that the
argument of knowledge versus thought, so common in the earlier
years of the Basic College, is now seldom heard. It has been replaced by comments that it is difficult to get students to think
and that many of them seem incapable of it.

Yet the pseudo-conflict does continue to plague us in more
subtle ways. This will be made evident in our following discus-

sion of a variety of efforts related to the study of the objective of
critical thinking.

Critical Thinking In and About
Objective Examinations

The citizen who casts his vote for one of several candidates for
public office may have thought long and intelligently about his
choice prior to making his mark on the printed ballot. On the
other hand, he may follow his father, employer, or labor union
leader in voting a straight ticket, or he may make selections
based upon momentary urges unclear even to himself. His X on
the ballot does not reveal the basis for his choice.

Likewise, an objective examination can pose questions which
evoke thought, but from the mark made on the answer sheet
there is no assurance that thought has taken place. If a question
on an objective examination is constructed to require more than
rote recall of previously presented information, there is a wishful
tendency to assume that choice of the right answer evidences
ability to carry through the thought process envisaged when the
item was written. Some investigations carried on by Leichty [1]
and Nelson conclusively demonstrated the over-optimism of this
assumption.

The procedure required students, shortly after the completion
of a comprehensive examination, to verbalize to a tape recorder
their choices of selected items and the reasons for them. Admittedly the situation was somewhat artificial, but students appeared to adjust to it readily and their recorded commentary
has the ring of sincerity to it. We are convinced that we obtained
valid samples of the way in which students think about the problems posed by objective test questions.

For some of the abler students the thought process closely
duplicated what was anticipated when the questions were prepared. For others, the selection of an answer was a haphazard
procedure dependent on recognition of familiar words or
phrases, or on a reaction to altogether irrelevant relationships

noted between the question and the various responses. Correct answers based on invalid reasoning or lack of it and incorrect answers based on incorrect assumptions or misinformation were frequent. Some students operated on the assumption that one either knows the answer or doesn't and either could not or would not attempt to organize and apply their knowledge to reason through to an answer. No wonder that some students characterize examinations which require thought as "guessing games!"

In some cases students jumped at answers and then tried to rationalize their choice or contented themselves with the remark "that just seems right." Decisions were sometimes reached by elimination with no evident assurance that the choice was truly correct. Series of items based on a single passage or problem were often seen as unrelated, with answers selected to later items contradicting earlier selections. The most discomforting finding was the total inability of some students to engage in a pattern of reasoning or even to realize that this was possible.

One index of the instability of choice was that only about 70 per cent of the choices made during the oral reworking of the items coincided in correctness or incorrectness with the earlier choices on the examination. As was to be expected, the better students tended to be more consistent than the poorer students, but not to an extent that was at all satisfying. It was of interest to us that Eells,[2] in an unpublished study of the same type made at the University of Chicago, reported findings almost identical with ours. The study by Bloom and Broder,[3] also made at the University of Chicago, provided further confirmation of some of our tentative conclusions about the inadequacy of the problem-solving processes of students.

Much as we continue to be disturbed about these findings, we cannot feel that the blame rests entirely on the students. It was evident that for many of the students the task of thinking through to an answer, rather than recalling one, was a novel experience. Indeed, one of the most recurrent criticisms culled from our senior surveys, reported elsewhere in this volume, is that Basic College examinations are irrelevant to the courses. By this the seniors mean, as many definitely stated in their comments, that the examinations contain questions for which the course did not provide the answers. One senior elaborated by noting, "I received A's from my instructors so I should know. True, I got A's on the examination but that was just luck!" Despite our concern about critical thinking, we have not been uniformly successful in making students aware of it. Neither have we been entirely unsuccessful in our efforts as some other evidence demonstrates.

In the early years of the Basic College, the year comprehensive examinations then required were divided into two parts. The first part was primarily a test of knowledge of facts, principles, and concepts. The second part required the application of this knowledge in situations selected to be new to the majority of students. Since, as we have already emphasized, productive thinking cannot proceed in the face of ignorance, the students who performed poorly on Part I did poorly on Part II. However, many students who did well on Part I were unable to maintain their achievement on Part II. Knowing the facts is not enough!

At that time there were two science courses: Physical Science and Biological Science. The former was essentially a factually-oriented survey. The latter course openly and repeatedly invited the student to think things through for himself. We thought that a survey of the achievement of entering freshmen paired with their later performance at the completion of basic courses would be of interest to the staff of each course. This particular study proceeded by administering complete comprehensive examinations to entering students and the same examinations later at the completion of the respective courses. The general pattern revealed respectable gains in knowledge items and lesser but still significant gains in thought and application items.

In the case of the two science courses, we found that the Biological Science students demonstrated the most favorable pat-

tern, with gains on number of correct answers in critical thinking being essentially equal to the gains in knowledge. In Physical
Science the students showed no gain in critical thinking and a
raw score gain in knowledge markedly less than that of the
Biological Science students. Admittedly such comparisons of raw
score gains between two different tests are precarious. Nevertheless, the results were certainly consistent with the hypothesis
that planned emphasis on critical thinking does make a difference and that such emphasis need not be at the expense of gains
in knowledge.

Our results were not welcomed by the staffs of the courses.
Some of the Physical Science instructors found other and more
ego-satisfying interpretations based on such diverse factors as
the inadequate mathematical background of the students, the
relative difficulty of the courses, and the irrelevance of the
examination to the purposes of the course. The real issue of
whether anything should be done to adjust the course in the light
of these facts and factors was largely ignored.

Some College Teachers Get Concerned

The interest of the Science staff in critical thinking was reflected in the doctoral dissertations and several related articles
by three members of the staff. Mason [4] studied scientific attitudes, viewing them as necessary preconditions and concomitants
of scientific thinking. Using an experimental procedure contrasted with the usual "discipline" approach in both lectures and
laboratory, he pre-tested and post-tested. Gains in scientific attitude and in scientific thinking were in the desired direction and,
viewing the results in their entirety, somewhat greater gains were
shown by students in the experimental group. Experimental and
traditional approaches were essentially equally effective in pro-
ducing gains in knowledge.

In another study by Solomon [5] the ability to use the scientific
method of problem solving was related to mental "rigidity" and
comprehensiveness. Rigidity, defined as "inability to change

one's mental set when the objective conditions demand it, and inability to rearrange a mental field in which there are alternative solutions to a problem in order to solve that problem more efficiently," was found to interfere with scientific thinking. Rigidity was associated with narrow and isolated, rather than comprehensive, cognitive patterns—that is, the more rigid individuals were less able to see broad and general relationships. These characteristics were found to be operative not only in experimental situations but in the classroom where they affected the achievement of the critical thinking goals of the science course. This study is of particular interest because it approaches the very difficult problem of the relation of thinking ability to other traits of personality. Mayhew has something more to say on this matter in Chapter 14. Although only students were studied by Solomon, one cannot refrain from wondering whether a study of instructional staff in regard to this characteristic might not reveal similar results.

The Communications staff has always displayed interest in critical thinking as an objective and has maintained a unit dealing with it throughout the many changes that have been made in the course. The staff has also used critical thinking or aspects of it as one of the criteria used in evaluating a theme or speech. More recently, with the addition of listening to the communication skills, there has been some coordinated effort to define and evaluate student development in respect to "critical listening." This skill appears to depend on or involve critical thinking, but it is too soon to speak with any assurance about the nature of it. The experiences and findings of Irwin,[6] Palmer, Dow and others of our Communications Department indicate that listening is an identifiable skill and, like reading, writing, or speaking, may vary from apathetic awareness of words to active and thoughtful participation in the communicative process. There is also some evidence that improvement is possible, but listening is still more a matter of study than an accepted and attainable course objective.

The Social Sciences and the Humanities departments have not

been productive of formal studies of critical thinking, although, as indicated earlier, there has been an interest in the problem. Undoubtedly part of the problem lies in developing really good situations for the evocation of critical thinking, situations for which there is a defensible right answer, the choice of which indicates with reasonable frequency that a valid pattern of reasoning was followed. Critical thinking items in the tests in Social Science and Humanities have never been as clearly distinguishable as in Natural Science or Communication Skills.

Cooperation Among Colleges

The Basic College of Michigan State was one of the participating colleges in the Cooperative Study of Evaluation in General Education. Critical thinking became the central concern of the committees involved in this project. Evaluation instruments involving this outcome were constructed in each of the fields of Communications, Science, Social Science, and Humanities. A general test was also developed using neutral materials largely devoid of any specialized knowledge in any of these four fields. In all of these endeavors representatives of the Basic College and of the Office of Evaluation Services played a prominent part largely because of the long period of interest and activity with regard to the objective being clarified and evaluated.

One phase of this cooperative evaluation project involved the administration of the various tests of critical thinking to entering freshmen and again to these same students at later stages. To our gratification Basic College students registered gains over the freshman and sophomore years which compared very favorably with those found in other institutions. However, in fairness, it must be admitted that our students probably had more experience with examinations of this type than was true with many of the other students involved. Indeed, the examinations developed in the Cooperative Evaluation Study corresponded so closely to the examinations regularly developed for our courses that in one case the entire Study test was accepted by the course staff as a part of the final examination. Improvement in critical thinking as measured in this manner should not be entirely discounted on the basis of familiarity with test materials, for tests themselves do help to set as well as reflect instructional emphasis and tests themselves may be educational experiences.

Another interesting feature of our participation in this study involved the relationship found between the Test of Critical Thinking and grades in Basic and non-Basic courses. The correlation with the average grades in all Basics completed by the junior year was .62, whereas the corresponding correlation with the average of non-Basic course grades was only .15. This would seem to reflect greater attention to critical thinking in the Basic courses, although here again it must be kept in mind that examinations of a similar nature played a large role in the grade determination for the Basic courses.

Considering all of the data occurring from the Cooperative Evaluation Study and other ventures noted earlier, we felt justified in reaching the conclusion that our emphasis on critical thinking in courses and in examinations had achieved results in our students at least as good as that found in similar programs, although still considerably less than we had hoped for and considered possible.

Cooperation Among High Schools

Somewhat as an aftermath of our extensive involvement in the cooperative venture among colleges, several members of the Office of Evaluation Services staff entered into an informal cooperative arrangement with a number of public school system curriculum and research directors. These directors shared our opinion that critical thinking was receiving less than its due in the classroom. With the cooperation of interested teachers from the several school systems, high school and junior high school level tests of problem solving (this term seemed more prevalent at these levels than critical thinking) were constructed. The development and use of the tests were seen as devices to interest teachers in the objective rather than as a means of evaluating student achievement. In fact and as usual, we found only slight gains recorded by student groups in most of the schools.

Faced with such evidence and realizing that current instructional practice seems to provide students with little opportunity for critical thinking, a number of teachers became interested in developing materials or approaches which would provide more extensive opportunity for students to engage in critical thinking. The initial attempts were in the direction of developing units based upon issues or problems which seemed to be particularly appropriate. Although the teachers seem to enjoy and profit from the experience, they found it difficult to make much use of these units in classes. With the necessity of covering specified blocks of material, the insertion of additional time-consuming units was impractical. Teachers, other than participants, were even less inclined to study and use the materials developed. We concluded that if more critical thinking was to be done it would have to be in relation to materials already a part of the curriculum.

Even so, we found another difficult issue. Teachers who became interested and attempted to encourage critical thinking too frequently found that their efforts were in vain. The injunction "Think" does not automatically elicit thinking. We did find that a tape recording of a class in which a teacher was particularly successful in getting students to do some original thinking was most provocative and helpful to teachers in demonstrating the meaning of critical thinking and in suggesting specific procedures for arousing it. Neither the instruction that prospective teachers have had in most of their academic preparation nor the courses in education required for certification provide teachers with the examples nor the experience which they need if they undertake seriously to encourage students to think rather than simply to learn and recall information.

A brief tour of elementary school teaching practices suggested to us that much of what is done there unintentionally but effectively squelches the normal curiosity of the child. His natural desire to know why and how is discouraged in favor of docilely proffering upon call by the teacher an approximation to the expected answer. Our committee of research and curriculum directors shares this view and accordingly has undertaken to develop some promotional pamphlets which will dramatize the importance, need, and possibilities of encouraging critical thinking in respect to a variety of simple situations commonly arising in classrooms at elementary and secondary school levels. (The irony of our recourse to propaganda in selling critical thinking has not been missed.) The group has also indicated particular concern that teachers should emphasize this objective in dealing with gifted students. One school system has already introduced a special class for the gifted using many of the ideas and materials developed by the committee.

A survey of gifted high school graduates made under the auspices of the committee emphasizes this need; one of the most frequently recurring comments of these graduates had to do with the lack of challenge which they had found in their courses. They reported that they found their real challenge in extra-curricular activities.

The Teachability of Thinking

There is no doubt that teachers vary greatly in their ability to provoke their students to think for themselves. Neither is there any doubt that teachers who turn their attention to the task can increase the amount of thinking done by students. To the recurring question of how to teach critical thinking, however, we have no simple nor sure answer.

For one thing, the question is wrongly put. Thinking is a personalized, internalized, and complex process which is not and probably never will be fully diagrammed. Intelligence certainly places some limits on ability to think. Interest, knowledge, and past experience also condition an individual as to what will cause him to think and how well he thinks. In some areas prejudice and values learned in the home or in a particular segment of society may impede or almost completely block critical thinking. We conclude that we cannot teach critical thinking. We can only try to introduce a variety of situations in the classroom to which ready answers are not available in the text, or to which the answers given can be brought into question in such a manner as to stimulate some of the students to attempt to provide their own. No one situation is likely to so stimulate all students, but if enough such situations are provided most students will ultimately be stimulated. The student who is frequently motivated to think and who has some opportunity to become self-critical about the processes and results of his thinking may learn to think more effectively.

Nevertheless, poor practices in arriving at conclusions can as readily become habitual as good ones. The teacher should help each student to become aware of his errors. In the attempt to do this and provide some ready tools, some programs have introduced rules of critical thinking and the technical terms of logic such as assumptions, hypotheses, and the various types of syllogisms. Such evidence as we have seen has invariably shown no advantage in a formal course in logic or thinking in respect to the growth of critical thinking about the materials in other courses, or practical problems arising in life. There is real value in becoming aware of assumptions, of the need for and relevance of evidence, of the formulation and testing of hypotheses—but these terms and concepts are better introduced gradually and naturally as students engage in thinking. One of the most effective teachers that we have seen in encouraging critical thinking consciously avoided the use of all such terms until students either introduced them or a particular situation developed to which the term added further insight.

In their concern with covering the material at hand, teachers often lose sight—and hence so do their students—of the real nature and purpose behind that material. Students are more likely to be stimulated to think about material at hand if it can be introduced in relation to a problem having meaning to them.

Frequently this is exactly the problem which gave rise to the material, yet in our preoccupation with the text it becomes the end rather than the means. The following three examples reinforce this point.

In one case a teacher sold on the importance of interpretation of data used a test involving many statements of a so-called "value" type which indicated actions that ought to be taken as a result of the evidence. These statements all involved assumptions of values not a part of the data and hence they were to be marked as "insufficient data" meaning that the data alone provided no basis for deciding as to the truth or falsity of the statements. The teacher instructed her students to the effect that any statement containing the words "should" or "ought" was a value statement and should be marked "insufficient data." Thus endeth critical thinking.

An English teacher, faced with taking up *Macbeth* the next Monday, raised the question as to how this might be taught to provoke critical thinking. Putting aside the issue of whether *Macbeth* was the most appropriate vehicle—for this was beyond the power of the teachers to decide—note was taken of the fact that Shakespeare as a truly great dramatist wrote for the stage and not for classroom reading. It was suggested that the television production of *Macbeth,* which had appeared just two weeks before, seemed to provide an obvious starting point. The teacher's reply was that the students had not been asked to view it because that didn't correspond with the schedule for starting *Macbeth.* Again the possibility of leading up to Macbeth by considering the role of ambition in our culture and whether it can be carried too far was likewise rejected because it would take an extra day or two which was not available.

To note another example: part of our folklore, learned by all school children, is that Columbus discovered America in 1492. We know this isn't true. Ignoring the Norsemen, one may still question whether landing on an island in the Caribbean should be so dignified. The further question of whether the event of an

Indian canoe reaching England in 1491 would have led to the "fact" that the Indians discovered Europe in 1491 raises some rather interesting issues with regard to ethnocentrism and racism as factors in determining what is historically "true."

Some courses and some materials are better adapted to stimulating the student to think than others. In certain courses for specialization in a particular field, the emphasis on achieving a significant mastery of a body of facts, principles, symbols, and techniques necessary for more advanced work may postpone until a more appropriate point the provision of opportunities for critical thinking. Any teacher willing to do some thinking himself can find at hand many opportunities to stimulate his students to strive for insights, understandings, and relations beyond the memorizing of the facts presented. To accomplish this takes time; time for students to think and time for the teacher to become aware of what the student is thinking. As our recorded interviews indicate, we frequently fool ourselves into believing that our thought processes are duplicated in the minds of our students. They seldom are.

In education generally and certainly in the Basic College, despite its avowed and evident concern with critical thinking, the rigid prescription of too much content tends to minimize understanding and thought in favor of mere knowledge. Classes tend to slide into a routine in which coverage of a block of material accompanied by precise interpretations by the instructor supersede or effectively bar any real involvement on the part of most students. Occasional teachers rise above this and most others can if they will. Despite all talk about improvement of teaching, the academic mores have thus far effectively tabooed the development of effective graduate or in-service training programs for college teachers in all but a few institutions.

That some greater emphasis on and achievement by students of the goal of critical thinking is possible and practical has been demonstrated by the Basic College as well as by other educational institutions. But anything like optimum results can come only through profound changes in the attitudes and in the practices of college teachers. Significant educational changes come slowly.

Notes

[1] V. E. Leichty, "What Makes a Test Item Bad?" *Journal of Educational Research,* October 1954, pp. 115–121; "Student Thinking on Items Involving Chronology," *Journal of Educational Research,* November 1954, pp. 187–194.

[2] K. W. Eells, "Problem-Solving Processes Used in Answering Selected Questions from the Social Science I Comprehensive Examination," unpublished doctoral dissertation, University of Chicago, 1948.

[3] Benjamin S. Bloom and Lois J. Broder, *Problem-Solving Processes of College Students* (Chicago: University of Chicago Press, 1950).

[4] J. M. Mason, "An Experimental Study in the Teaching of Scientific Thinking in Biological Science at the College Level," unpublished doctoral dissertation, Michigan State College, 1951.

[5] Marvin D. Solomon, "Studies in Mental Rigidity and the Scientific Method," *Science Education,* October 1952, pp. 240–247, 263–269; March 1953, pp. 121–131.

[6] Charles E. Irwin, "An Analysis of Certain Aspects of a Listening Training Program Conducted Among College Freshmen at Michigan State College," unpublished doctoral dissertation, Michigan State College, 1954.

14

LEWIS B. MAYHEW

And in Attitudes

The Importance of Attitudes in the Basic College

The committee recommendation on the establishment of the Basic College included suggested course objectives for the proposed seven areas of study. These objectives were divided into three general categories: knowledge and understanding, skills and abilities, and attitudes and appreciations. The latter category included:

1. an appreciation of the role speaking and writing play in a democracy.

2. perception of aesthetic values in nature.

3. appreciation of the orderliness of nature.

4. an attitude of willingness to accept and use scientific facts in the solution of social problems and in planning courses of action.

5. a willingness to accept responsibility for intelligent participation in family and community life.

6. to develop an attitude of sympathetic understanding toward contemporary ways of life other than our own.

7. an appreciation of the kinds and degrees of pleasure and meaning found in art at various levels, from the passingly popular to the classics which offer more intense and renewable enjoyment.

There is nothing unique about the list but it underscores the point that from its inception the Basic College assumed an

214

obligation for objectives beyond the purely intellectual. This concern has continued. When the Basic College program was reorganized into four courses, the revised statement of purpose included:

1. understanding and appreciation of the traditions, institutions, and cultural experiences of man and their significance in dealing with modern problems.
2. understanding of, and active belief in, the value of
    a. a genuine concern for the welfare of all men.
    b. the dignity of the individual and his right to growth and expression in a free society.
    c. living by consistent principles rather than by simple expediency.

These and similar goals have subsequently been incorporated into the specific purposes of the several Basic College courses. How they are viewed, of course, ranges from the cynical view that they represent mere window dressing to the idealists' conviction that they represent the really valid guideposts for the organizing of general education. The majority of instructors have given no overt attention to influencing attitudes. A typical reaction is that attitudes are important, but in the absence of knowledge as to defensible means of influencing attitudes it is assumed that whatever changes come about result from changes in knowledge and understanding. Associated with this view is a profound skepticism about and a lack of interest in any attempt to appraise attitudinal changes. Partly because of this indifference and partly because of the technical difficulties involved, there has been no continuing program of attitude measurement.

Difficulties in Appraising Attitudes

Attitudes, values, and personal adjustment are all internalized and their existence can only be inferred from overt behavior. An attitude, for example, has been defined as "an emotionalized tendency to act for or against something." Its existence and its nature may be inferred either from what a person says or from what he does. Such inferences are subject to error. Individuals frequently do not wish others to know how they feel or what they believe, and so they act or respond in ways misleading to the observer. The individual may even deceive himself as to how he feels about many matters. The task of cutting through such inhibitions to obtain valid information is a difficult if not impossible process.

The scientific study of feeling is such a recent development that its most elaborate and effective techniques are rejected by large numbers of students, teachers, and parents. Administrative considerations and expense commonly dictate the use of short answer questionnaires, and objective type tests for attitude study. Yet to many people, the idea that a person's feeling about God could be even approximately inferred from his responses on an I.B.M. answer sheet is repulsive. This distrust of attitude measurement is intensified if appraisals of attitudes reveal trends contrary to expectations. For example, a study which reveals that a course is strongly disliked by many students is likely to be viewed with skepticism by the teacher of that course.

Added to these difficulties is the ethical problem regarding attitudes. In American ideology an individual's feelings and opinions are private. A constitutional provision safeguards the individual's religious and political beliefs. Yet the school does try to alter beliefs and it is criticized or praised by those who believe it has succeeded or failed. This dilemma places the teacher in a difficult situation. He is concerned with students' attitudes, but he is also concerned because manipulation of human beings is contrary to his own value system. Even if he accumulates evidence on attitudinal change or the lack of it, he hesitates to use the evidence in an evaluation of individual student performance. In the Basic College this situation has been rationalized by permitting inquiry but insisting that the resulting data can only be used to study group changes or to counsel individual students. A student's status is never affected by his attitudes expressed in connection with an appraisal project. The student, however, is not always convinced of this.

In spite of these difficulties several attempts have been made to study the affective qualities of students. These have ranged from obtaining evidence about the major attitudinal objectives of the Basic College to finding out student feelings about specific aspects of the Basic College program.

Attitudes Toward All Basic College Courses

The first such study involved the attitudes or values common to all seven of the Basic College courses. These, as they were finally formulated by an inter-departmental committee, were stated as a series of ten continua:

1. Belief in discussion and majority decision *versus* acceptance of arbitrary action on the part of the minority. According to the thinking which led to the establishment of this continuum, extreme insistence on majority decision in every situation can be as harsh and as arbitrary as the authoritarian rule of a single individual.

2. Rejection of all authority *versus* uncritical acceptance of authority. Some persons feel secure only when guided by authority, regardless of its competence. These may be contrasted with those who consider all men's opinions about every subject to be equally valid.

3. Active participation in democratic processes *versus* indifference and non-participation. The one extreme represents continual participation in such varied activities that effectiveness is not possible in any of them. The other extreme is illustrated by complete withdrawal from society.

4. Respect for the general welfare *versus* unconcern for the rights of society or of elements of society. This principle is perhaps most clearly illustrated by rabid internationalists at one extreme, with the equally rabid isolationists or sectionalists occupying the opposite position.

5. Respect for and demand for evidence *versus* uncritical ac-

ceptance of unvalidated statements. The scholar who, while working diligently on his specialty, is never willing to publish because he always needs just a little more evidence represents one extreme. His counterpart is the person who is willing to accept almost any plausible-sounding statement.

6. Concern for, and interest in, all fields *versus* limitation of interest to a specialized field. Worshippers of vocation, money, or some other single, all-pervasive life purpose exemplify one extreme of this principle. Those who become so much interested in so many fields that intelligent appreciation is possible in none of them represent the other.

7. Open-mindedness *versus* uncritical adherence to law and custom. Those to whom novelty is the supreme value might be said to demonstrate an extreme of open-mindedness. Those who always seek to keep the status quo in all things illustrate the opposite.

8. Active concern for others *versus* self-centeredness or indifference. Such concern for others that one would be willing to make every sacrifice, even that of life, in order that others might live, is contrasted with resentment at others' good fortune.

9. Definite goals or philosophy *versus* simple expediency. If the hypothesis that people respond to many situations according to a few fairly stable principles is accepted, then one extreme of this category might be illustrated by conscious, literal adherence to those principles in every circumstance. Habitual response to situations only in terms of transient factors intrinsic to each situation typifies the opposite.

10. Acceptance of responsibility for decision and action *versus* indecision. While some men desire to accept or assume responsibility for action in all matters regardless of the appropriateness of their doing so, others constantly practice procrastination and are reluctant to assume any responsibility or to reach any decisions.

The Office of Evaluation Services, with the help of many

faculty members, prepared a situational type test to measure student changes with respect to these continua. Situations were drafted in which personal conflict was explicit. Several possible responses to each situation were provided with the student expected to accept, reject or remain ambivalent to the response according to his own feelings. For example, one such situation and its response was:

In Hungary, the government decided that the schools, traditionally the responsibility of the Roman Catholic Church, should be brought under state control. The Cardinal, head of the Hungarian Church, opposed the decision and ordered the bishops who managed the schools, and the priests who taught in them, to resist the order. For this and for other acts against the government, the head of the Hungarian Church was tried for treason and sentenced to life imprisonment. Many people, the world over, criticized the action of the Hungarian government. A great many people, however, defended the civil action on the ground that church opposition to bringing schools under state control actually was against the best interests of the state and should be punished.

36. The trend against church control of education in Hungary was undoubtedly instigated by Communists in Russia.
(This statement was designed to give an indication of students' attitudes toward evidence.)

37. If church control of schools has not worked perfectly in Hungary, some other arrangement should be attempted.
(This was designed to reveal the degree of open-mindedness students maintain.)

38. Relations between church and state in many European countries are so confused that we Americans can never understand them well enough to form intelligent opinions.
(This also was designed to show students' attitudes toward evidence.)

39. If the majority of Hungarians desired the Catholic Church to control schools, the government should not allow any non-Catholic schools to operate.
(This statement was written to reveal the degree to which students favor majority rule.)

40. There is a definite limit to the kinds of measures the Hungarian people would be justified in using to secure the release of the Cardinal.

(This was designed to test attitudes toward participation in public affairs.)

41. The state can never have sufficient evidence to justify a charge that a church official's service to his church is treason against his country.

(This, again, is supposed to test students' regard for evidence.)

42. Laymen were not justified in interesting themselves in the control of education, traditionally the concern of the Roman Catholic Church.

(This statement was designed to indicate students' attitudes toward individual participation in affairs of interest to society.)

This inventory was administered to an entire freshman class and as a post-test to a selected sample of students who had taken three terms of the course Effective Living. Students demonstrated changes on all ten categories in what might be conceived of as the desirable direction. Thus, they moved toward majority decision, criticalness of authority, active participation, respect for the general welfare, demand for evidence, catholicity of interests, open-mindedness, active concern for others, a definite philosophy and a willingness to accept responsibility. Further detailed study with this instrument was precluded by personnel changes, resulting disinterest, and the press of other matters.

Attitudes Toward Comprehensive Examinations

Of major significance to the faculty of the Basic College has been student feeling about the program. The introduction of a requirement of courses in general education for all students and the use of comprehensive examinations in appraising student achievement were certain to cause marked reactions. If student reactions were generally favorable, the assumption was that the program would have that much more chance of success. If the reactions were antagonistic, such feelings might markedly affect student achievement.

The first definite attempt to explore this area was in connection with an overall analysis of the comprehensive examination program.[1] Opinionnaires were sent to students currently in the Basic College, students who had finished the Basic College, and faculty members in the Basic College. Both students and former students found much to praise and much to criticize in the comprehensive examination program. The vast majority liked the feature of credit by examination. They liked a single test common to all sections of a course. They did not like their entire grade based on one examination; they felt that the classroom teacher ought to have some hand in determining grades. Students, as a group, did not object to objective-type examinations, although women disliked the objective tests much more frequently than men. While students did not feel that the examination was too difficult, over half of them did not understand the inclusion in the examination of new situations requiring utilization of their knowledge. The general feeling seemed to be approval of the ideas of a comprehensive examination, but distrust and even marked disapproval of some of its associated features.

One of the issues concerning the comprehensive examination program was the degree to which classroom motivation was affected by the instructor not wielding the grading prerogative. To investigate this matter adequately was nearly impossible. However, certain facets of the question were studied. One involved the relationship between student attitudes toward comprehensive examinations and certain other variables regarding students. For example, we compared the attitudes of students taking a comprehensive examination after three terms of a course with those of students who took only one term's work. To study this, two instruments were developed. One was a short attitude scale utilizing a series of selected statements scaled from unfavorable to favorable. Students were asked to check those statements with which they agreed. The second instrument used was a multiple choice test for knowledge about the comprehensive examination system. The sources for this knowledge were the various published documents available to students.

These two tests were administered to students in the first and third terms of all Basic College courses in Fall Term 1949. Then the various relationships were studied and yielded the following generalizations:

1. Students' attitudes ranged from a distinctly unfavorable to a highly favorable point of view. The mean scores for students in the various Basic courses were all slightly in the favorable direction.

2. Students' attitudes were not related to the number of terms' credits they had gained by taking a comprehensive examination early, nor to the course they had elected as their extra Basic course.

3. The age of students was unrelated to their attitudes, but sex was. Female students were distinctly less favorable toward the comprehensive examinations. Since the faculty is chiefly a male one, it can be suspected that female students recognize their loss of advantage from instructor grading.

4. Females who had received credit by examination had more favorable attitudes than did females who had not. For men this particular comparison revealed no such differences.

5. The higher a student's grades on comprehensive examinations, the more favorable were his attitudes toward them.

6. Students' attitudes toward the comprehensive examination were unrelated to their knowledge about the examination program. This particular point has been established in so many attitude studies as to bring into serious question just how attitudes are to be affected if they are unrelated to knowledge.

7. Students did not know very much about the reasons for and the features of the examination program, although this knowledge did increase in proportion to the number of comprehensive examinations taken.

Attitudes Toward the Goals of General Education

It has frequently been charged that students were so vocationally oriented as to resent being required to take courses in the liberal arts or general education. To determine whether this was so, a questionnaire was developed asking students to judge the relative value of twenty-six accepted goals of collegiate education. Sixteen of these were relevant to general education and ten to specialized or vocational education. The instrument was administered to several randomly selected groups of students during 1953, 1954, and 1955. Typically, these students ranked such goals of general education as critical thinking, getting along with people, adequacy in communications, emotional and social adjustment ahead of more vocationally oriented objectives. Since the same results were obtained for freshmen, for transfer students, for sophomores, and for seniors, we were convinced that these students were substantially in favor of the purposes of the Basic College for the first two years of college.[2] The reactions of graduates reported by Dressel in Chapter 6 confirm this interpretation.

Attitudes Toward the Freshman Year

Three other studies need to be mentioned which bear on the problem of the students' view of the Basic College. The first of these was made in connection with the annual Student-Principal Conference. At this conference principals visit their former students, then discuss with the faculty the reactions of these students to their high school preparation and their reception at Michigan State. To make the collection of these reactions more systematic, a questionnaire was developed by the Office of High School Cooperation and the Office of Evaluation Services and administered to 1,926 freshmen in the fall of 1951. These students believed that Michigan State could have helped their adjustment to college by a number of methods.

They wanted more complete orientation to the campus and to the Basic College and fewer tests during Orientation Week. They wanted more time to see counselors, and more effective help from their enrollment officers in selecting courses of study. They indicated a desire for better matched roommates, more advance information regarding housing, and more adequately regulated quiet hours. They wanted simplification of registration procedures and more assistance for freshmen in registering. Courses, they thought, could be improved if teachers would orient students more fully to the demands and purposes of the courses. They offered a number of suggestions for improving adjustment which ranged from helping students know more people to de-emphasizing football (even at Michigan State University).

Attitudes Toward Specific Basic College Courses

Using a scale constructed similarly to the one used for student attitudes toward comprehensive examinations, a study was made of student attitudes toward the course Effective Living.[3] Student reaction to Effective Living was typically slightly more favorable than unfavorable. When various subgroups of the total population studied were compared several items of interest emerged:

1. Children of professional, sub-professional, and managerial homes were more favorable to the course than were children of laboring and farming homes.

2. Students who signed their names to the questionnaire showed significantly better scores, i.e. more favorable attitudes, than students who responded anonymously.

3. Students who ranked their instructors high on an Instructor Rating Scale showed more favorable attitudes toward the course than those who ranked their teachers down.

4. Students from small classes tended to like the course more than did students from larger classes.

5. Students earning A or B grades in Effective Living liked the course better than D or F students.

6. Students who had finished the course were more favorable to it than students who were still in the course.

Significant as are students' attitudes toward the program, of much more importance are their attitudes about other matters susceptible of modification by the program. Coupled with the increased significance, however, is increased difficulty in studying them. It is here that the full intensity of the matters discussed in the beginning of this chapter are felt. Thus the discussion which follows should be read with these difficulties and limitations in mind.

The Effect of Specific Courses on Student Attitudes

One of the first large attempts to study attitudes as outcomes of the Michigan State program was made by Dahnke.[4] He attempted to discover, among other things: 1) what changes occur in the adjustment, attitudes, interests and values of students in the course Effective Living, and 2) the relationships between a student's knowledge of the materials of the course Effective Living and those affective qualities.

In the fall of 1948 and in the following spring students were tested at the beginning and at the end of the course with several measures. The following tests were used: the *Minnesota Multiphasic Personality Inventory,* which obtains evidence on certain psychological variables such as depression, paranoia, or hypomania; a prejudice scale; an *Opinion Survey,* which elicits attitudes toward minority groups; the *Kuder Preference Record,* which obtains indications of vocational interest; and the *Allport-Vernon Study of Values,* which indicates students' relative adherence to certain major value orientations such as theoretical, economic or power orientations. The course in Effective Living was of such nature as to involve and possibly affect the qualities involved in each of the measures used. From the data Dahnke advanced the tentative conclusions that, during the year in Effective Living, the students 1) bettered their personal adjustment, 2) became more friendly toward minority group members, 3) maintained their original interests, and 4) altered their values only slightly.

The next, and perhaps most important, problem considered by this research was the relationship between attitudes, interests, values, and personal adjustment, and measures of knowledge in the course. In general, there were group changes in amounts of prejudice and in degree of personal adjustment over the year, but these changes were unrelated to growth in knowledge of the course. Interests, also, seemed to be unchanged by acquisition of more knowledge. The causes of those changes which were detected and the relation to those changes of the knowledge gained in the course were and ever shall remain unanswered questions.

In the Department of Natural Science various concepts are taught which seem likely to question some of the students' deeply-held beliefs. During the second term of that course in 1955–56, a pilot study was conducted to determine the effect student exposure to the concepts of organic evolution had on 1) their belief in evolution, and 2) their belief in the Bible.

One hundred and three students were included in the study, which was conducted on a pre-post-test basis. The scales developed by L. L. Thurstone as part of his work on the measurement of social attitudes were used. The results show that before any instruction or assignments were made the attitude of the class toward evolution was neutral, while their attitude toward the Bible was one of strong belief. In terms of the attitude scale where the "neutral" position ranges between 5.0 and 5.9, the "belief in" position between 6.0 and 7.4 and the "strong belief" position between 7.5 and 11.0, the students averaged 5.26 as their attitude toward evolution and 8.62 in their attitude toward the Bible. Upon the completion of the term's work and with due recognition being given to the factor of reliability of the post-test's results, the students averaged 6.34 in their attitude toward evolution and 8.37 in their attitude toward the Bible. The pilot study showed that exposure of the class of freshman students to the concepts of evolution changed their belief in evolution decidedly, but that their belief in the Bible, during the same period, remained strong.

The Effect of the Basic College
on Student Attitudes

As indicated elsewhere, Michigan State was active in the Cooperative Study of Evaluation in General Education. In implementing the work of that undertaking several rather important projects involving attitudes were accomplished. One of the instruments developed in the Study was an *Inventory of Beliefs* which consisted of 120 statements of pseudo-rational generalizations, over-generalizations, and statements of stereotyped beliefs. Students taking the test were asked either to strongly agree or agree, to disagree or to strongly disagree. This *Inventory* was administered to a large group of freshmen and to a comparable but smaller group of upperclassmen. While one cannot know whether the Basic College was responsible for differences in the beliefs held by these two groups, the differences and similarities are interesting as suggesting what might be happening to our students. To check on this more precisely would require using the instrument on the same group of students as freshmen and as last term sophomores.

In the area of the humanities several well-marked differences were found. Fifty per cent of the freshmen believed that "Europeans criticize the United States for materialism but such criticism is only to cover up the realization that American culture is far superior to their own," while 22 per cent of the upperclassmen believed this. Seventy-seven per cent of the freshmen believed that "There is only one real standard in judging art works—each to his own taste," while 57 per cent of the upperclassmen did. Twenty-six per cent of the freshmen accepted the statement "Why study the past when there are so many problems of the present to be solved," while only 8 per cent of the upperclassmen took this viewpoint. On all nineteen questions which pertained to the humanities there was either no change or change in the direction implied by the examples cited.

There were thirty-eight questions relating to the social

sciences. Again the pattern was marked in that the percentage of students accepting these over-generalizations decreased between the freshman and upperclass groups. There was, however, one interesting exception. Thirty-one per cent of the freshmen thought "The predictions of economists about the future of business are no better than guesses," while 75 per cent of the upperclassmen thought so.

There were fourteen statements about the natural sciences; a larger proportion of both upperclassmen and freshmen accepted a larger number of these than statements from the first two fields. For example, 81 per cent of freshmen and of upperclassmen believed "There are a lot of things in this world that will never be explained by science." Ninety per cent of freshmen and 84 per cent of upperclassmen believed "The scientist that really counts is the one who turns theories into practical use." Forty-three per cent of freshmen and 68 per cent of upperclassmen believed that "Science is infringing upon religion when it attempts to delve into the origin of life itself." These sentiments are especially interesting in view of the scientific orientation of the entire University.

Responses to the nineteen statements of general opinion showed considerable variation in the kinds of differences between the two groups. For example, fewer upperclassmen than freshmen accepted the idea that "We are finding out today that liberals really are soft-headed, gullible, and potentially dangerous." On the other hand, more upperclassmen than freshmen thought that "As young people grow up they ought to get over their radical ideas."

The thirty questions involving ethics revealed that both freshmen and upperclassmen had faith in a personal God, faith in individualism, and faith in a rather rugged brand of capitalism. A few items are exemplary. Sixty-six per cent of the freshmen and 69 per cent of the upperclassmen believed that "There is a source of knowledge that is not dependent upon observation." Seventy-seven and 81 per cent, respectively, thought that "In our society, a person's first duty is to protect from harm himself and those dear to him." Eighty-nine and 57 per cent thought "When things seem black, a person should not complain, for it may be God's will." Eighty-seven and 88 per cent thought "There are times when a father, as head of the family, must tell the other family members what they can do and cannot do." Ninety-five and 92 per cent thought "Children should learn to respect and obey their teachers."

While the changes in opinion about specific statements are interesting, the *Inventory* was designed to yield an even more significant index about students. The instrument was based in part on the theories of Adorno and others in the University of California studies on Authoritarianism.[5] According to these studies, there are some persons who are consistently rigid, non-adaptive, anxious, uncomfortable, egocentric, and ethnocentric, and who reveal these traits by acceptance of a relatively large number of stereotyped statements. Those who reject a large number might be described as comfortable, adaptive, flexible, and out-going. If this rationale is valid and if the *Inventory* does assess the trait, then the generalization can be made that Basic College students are more authoritarian when they start school than are students from twelve out of thirteen other institutions. During the first year, however, the complexion of the group changes and it becomes slightly less authoritarian.

This profile of students as they enter Michigan State seems reasonable in the light of what we know about our students and in the light of what we are learning about the authoritarian person. Authoritarianism appears to be related to high ethnocentrism, religious fundamentalism (regardless of denomination), conservative economic doctrine, interest in power and status, and vocational choices along practical rather than abstract lines. A large number of our students come from Detroit and vicinity, but the majority come from small towns and rural areas. Although there are many Jews and Catholics, the fundamentalist Protestant religions are strong in Michigan. Most of our students still come to us to receive a practical, specialized education in some vocational field. The fact that these students do change during their Basic College experience is taken as a rather significant finding.

This same *Inventory* has been administered to several groups as a pre-test and as a post-test at the end of varying periods of time. Students at the end of a one-term experimental class in Social Science did not earn significantly different scores. Student scores did shift about two points after one full year in college, and about two more points after another full year. From this evidence we can infer that, while the traits measured by the *Inventory* are relatively stable and probably deeply embedded in the individual's personality, they are some what modified—whether it be by education, maturation, or just getting away from home we do not know.

Perhaps the first generalization about the measurement of attitudes is that the number of studies to date does not reflect the importance assigned to attitudes by the Basic College faculty. This is understandable in view of the difficulties in attitude measurement. However, since attitudes and values continue to remain so central among the educational outcomes of the Basic College, this very lack might serve as stimulation for deeper and more searching inquiry among all manner of affective factors.

Implications for the Future

Our experiences as described here and in other chapters indicate a need to probe further the expressed attitudes regarding the examination system, the teaching in the Basic College courses, and the Basic College courses. What factors, for example, cause some students to view the teaching in the Basics as less adequate than upper school teaching? Why is knowledge about examinations unrelated to students' attitudes regarding them? Why, in view of the time expended on the matter of undergraduate teaching and examining in the Basic College, is a significant minority of students skeptical about their values?

In Effective Living it was found that knowledge in the course was unrelated to changes in prejudice. Since this is consistent with many other findings, it gives rise to serious questions. If courses seek to inculcate knowledge and if acquisition of knowledge does not effect attitudes, should attitudinal objectives be rejected? Or, if the objectives be retained, should ways be sought which actually have some effect on students' attitudes? It is known, for example, that some techniques of teaching which seem almost non-rational in their operation do make differences in how students feel. Asking students to play roles of minority group members, subjecting them to pointedly dramatic experiences, or allowing them the freedom of a counseling interview, have all been tried. To what extent could these be woven into the fabric of all of the Basic College courses, and to what extent can the results be studied?

Notes

[1] *Comprehensive Examinations in a Program of General Education* (East Lansing: Michigan State College Press, 1949).

[2] Willard G. Warrington, John W. Kidd and Harold H. Dahnke, "General Education—Its Importance During the First Two Years of College," *Junior College Journal,* December 1955, pp. 228–232.

[3] Laurence S. Cooke, "An Analysis of Certain Factors Which Affect Student Attitudes Toward a Basic College Course, Effective Living," doctoral dissertation, Michigan State College, 1952.

[4] Harold L. Dahnke, Jr., "Analysis of the Testing Program in the Department of Effective Living," doctoral dissertation, Western Reserve University, 1950.

[5] T. W. Adorno, et al., *The Authoritarian Personality* (New York: Harper & Bros., 1950).

15

PAUL L. DRESSEL and
LEWIS B. MAYHEW

And There Should Be More

This chapter title is ambiguous by intent. It refers to the need for more or perhaps greater change in encouraging critical thinking and in influencing attitudes. It refers as well to "evaluation" or "research." One purpose in undertaking this volume was that of assessing our accomplishment as a basis for planning further research. In several cases the attempt to summarize past research revealed gaps or raised questions with which the writer felt compelled to deal before continuing. The experience of summarizing our efforts has added something to our knowledge and suggested further problems. There will be more research, quite likely on each of the topics discussed in the various chapters. The bodies of data from which Carlin and Warrington gave preliminary reports in their respective chapters are still being analyzed and should be productive of two significant reports. Studies of our examinations will certainly continue.

Particularly, however, we are intrigued with the studies of attitudes, the extent of change in attitudes, and implications of these for instruction. Our failure with tests used to date to find any relationship between critical thinking abilities and rigidity also stirs our curiosity. What little we have in the way of evidence on these matters only whets our appetite.

We have noted earlier that when those students who make higher instructor grades than examination grades are equated in intelligence to those with the opposite pattern, the latter group scores significantly higher on the *Inventory of Beliefs* than does the former. In interviews with students receiving higher instructor grades, these students reflected fear of the examination. They argued that it did not correspond to class work, that it was too ambiguous, too long, and required too much reading. These students blamed external factors for real or anticipated failure. The students with higher examination grades reflected some lack of interest in the Basic courses, particularly in the class work. They studied for the examination, having confidence that their ability would carry them through. They saw their performance in the course and in the examination as of their own making. We speculate that many teachers prefer students who conform, who accept what is being taught without question, seek to determine the wishes of the teachers, and demonstrate some anxiety as to how they are performing.

The relative independence and adaptability of students who score high on the *Inventory of Beliefs*—i.e., the non-rigid persons —may also be seen in another context. In 1955 one section of the first term in Social Science was taught by what might be described as a non-directive, student-centered, permissive technique. Students were told that they would be held responsible for the readings of the course on the term-end examination. Aside from that requirement, there would be no instructor-posed demands throughout the term. They could come to class or not, as they saw fit. They could discuss whatever they wished or they could sit silently if that was their need at the moment. The teacher would be present but would be at the service of the students. He would make no assignments, begin no discussions, give no tests, and assign no grades. All these were to be responsibilities of the students.

As the term progressed, some students adjusted to this extreme variation from orthodox classroom procedure and reported that they enjoyed the freedom of choice it allowed them. Further, they did well on the final examination. Other students became more and more disturbed as the term wore on and manifested this either through apathy or through hostility toward the teacher, department, or system. Some of these students came to class every day for an entire term and never spoke. They complained of the threat of the impending examination and pleaded with the teacher to do something to help them prepare for it. The group which adjusted to the unstructured course scored significantly higher on the *Inventory of Beliefs* given as a pretest than did the group disturbed by the method.

With this experience as a guide, in 1956 a second experiment was conducted. This time twenty students were selected from five sections of Social Science on the basis of very high scores on the *Inventory of Beliefs*. These were formed into one section and were taught by the same non-directive techniques. They were allowed to discuss anything which was brought up and told to come to class or not, as they wished. This group, as a group, began after a day or so to make definite suggestions regarding what they might do. They realized that they would be held for the common term-end examination, so they worked out a rough schedule of readings which they could follow to know how they were doing.

None of the group took violent sides in a discussion but shared their ideas and accepted the ideas of others as each individual elected. They demonstrated none of the hostility toward the teacher, department, course or system that the low-scoring students in the previous experiment had. They said they viewed the class as an interesting experience in which they were happy to participate. During the entire term nothing seemed to excite the group except the suggestion that they should assign their own grades. One girl expressed the sentiment of the group when she said she didn't want the grade she would be forced to give herself. They were satisfied when the teacher told them that he would review their estimates and in discussion with the individual reconcile any divergence of judgment. The group performed outstandingly well on the term-end examination. Fifty per cent made B or higher on the examination, and 75 per cent made C + or higher. This is compared with the 30 per cent B or above that characterized the entire population of the course on Social Science that term.

In retrospect it would seem that these students were so adaptive that they could adjust quickly and with satisfaction to the experience of an unstructured class. It was as though they saw always what their goal was. If they could not achieve the goal through having a teacher tell them, they would find other means. They could accept such a new approach to teaching as an interesting experience in no sense threatening to them.

Conceptions of rigidity have been studied by other techniques than the *Inventory of Beliefs*. A well-known conception is that of Luchins, who developed a series of problems involving jars of water. Some of the problems could be solved only by rather complicated manipulations. Others, ostensibly of the same order, required relatively simple procedures. Students who, when first given the complicated problems, attempted to employ the same technique when faced with problems requiring only the simple procedure, were judged rigid. Students who could see through and adjust the solution employed to the problems were judged non-rigid and adaptable.

Using Luchins' technique for selecting rigid and non-rigid students, teachers in the Basic College Department of Natural Science have made several studies relevant to the material of this chapter. It has been found that there is a significant difference between rigid and non-rigid students with respect to their ability to use various aspects of the scientific method. Such abilities as those required 1) to recognize a logical hypothesis, 2) to recognize data supporting an hypothesis, 3) to recognize a valid experiment, or 4) to recognize a reasonable interpretation of the data, were tested in the context of materials from the biological sciences. In 24 of the 33 problems presented students, statistically significant differences in the anticipated direction

were found between the rigid and non-rigid student performance.[1]

In a second experiment using the same criterion of rigidity,
students were presented lists of interrelated terms and asked to
indicate how the terms were related. Students varied markedly
in their success with this task. Some made discrete comments
about each term, others perceived relationships between a few
terms, while still others were able to reduce all terms to a single
generalization. The degree of success in perceiving and express-
ing relationships was positively related to non-rigidity. Thus the
non-rigid students tended to see a greater number and greater
intensity of relationships than the rigid students.

A third experiment involved a classroom situation in which
students were pre-tested about the substance of an experiment to
be conducted. After several experiments the same test was again
administered. It was speculated that the non-rigid students
would achieve higher scores than the rigid students, due to their
greater ability to generalize. The results substantiated the expectations.

At the present time, of course, almost any college professor
who has thought about the matter can give common-sense answers about why these differences exist. Some students get along
with certain instructors but not with others. Some students'
minds seem unadaptable to certain kinds of abstract reasoning
but quite facile with others. Quite a few students get so worked
up about examinations that they leave school rather than face
the tension of taking tests. Some students just seem unhappy
with college work, while others seem bored with book work.

These common-sense "solutions" are really other ways of
describing the problem, but they do point to some possible explanations which are only now being explored by educational
and psychological research. Such research efforts have sought to
explain why some students, apparently quite intelligent, seem so
uncomfortable in certain educational situations; why some
students seem to profit from work with some professors but not

with others; and why some students view examinations as threats while others view them as opportunities.

Perhaps the most promising leads have come from various theories of personality. These all view the human being as a totality of interacting aspects. The intellects of students thus cannot be divorced from their emotions nor from their physical bodies. According to these theories, the individual may learn any of a variety of ways of responding to external reality. One child may develop fears and will typically respond to life defensively, while another will feel so safe and secure that he can tolerate almost any condition in which life places him. He further can modify himself without jeopardizing his essential self so as to profit from any context in which he finds himself. Such habits of behavior learned early are then reinforced by the individual's selection, out of the variety of experiences which surround him, of those experiences consistent with what he already knows or feels.

One significant theory which has emerged out of such speculation is the idea of rigidity as a pervasive personality characteristic. It has been suggested that some persons, because of multiple factors in their backgrounds, tend to become highly rigid in the way they respond to life. They see life as essentially threatening. They have learned a few patterns of response which are partly satisfying to them and they fear to deviate from these. They have learned, for example, that the safest response they can make toward anything new is aggression or withdrawal, or some other inappropriate response. Gradually such behavior becomes fixed and they act consistently in all situations.

Such college students can be described as rigid, compulsive individuals who never act spontaneously but always in terms of what they believe others expect them to do. They are conforming to the extent that they feel uncomfortable when they deviate from what they sense to be prevailing standards of conduct. They are threatened persons who feel that they must act aggressively in all situations except in the few in which they feel safe. They are inclined to be highly egocentric because they feel they must protect what they regard as weak selves. They are inclined to be highly ethnocentric because they derive security from feeling as one with a small group whose standards they understand. The possibility of their being other standards frightens them so much that they reject the possibility both intellectually and emotionally.

At the other end of the continuum are the non-rigid individuals. They might be described as relaxed and comfortable individuals. They feel sufficiently secure in themselves to be at home in almost any situation. They are adaptive, accepting life for what it is and being willing to adjust to it or to know why they will not adjust. They are outgoing persons who can accept differing points of view and ways of doing things as being not only natural but desirable. They lack the incapacitating anxiety characteristic of rigid students. Such people may be rather difficult for a society or a school to cope with. They may tend to be so unconcerned about conventional behavior or requirements as to cause genuine embarrassment to officials. As we have found out, students demonstrating these traits have some interesting things to say about the Basic College courses.

If this theory of rigidity or authoritarianism is a valid one and if it does, as our studies suggest, affect how students react to the Basic College curriculum, some serious implications are presented. One possible interpretation would hold that these personality characteristics are so deeply imbedded in an individual as to be immovable by routine educational methods. Such a thesis would see the traits forming within the first several years of an individual's life. By the time he reaches college these tendencies have been so reinforced by selected experiences that they are unchangeable.

If this interpretation is accepted, education may either ignore the problem, leaving the individual to succeed or fail as he will, or try to plan certain classes or learning situations in which the authoritarian person can function comfortably. If it does the former it must accept the responsibility for a number of capable students either dropping out of school or being distinctly uncomfortable and anxious while in school. If it does the latter, the administrative problems of devising special experiences for students with different personality orientations becomes an expensive and possibly unattainable goal. There is, of course, some precedent in special courses and sections for inept students. But the ethics and the procedures of screening students on intellectual grounds are at the present much more secure than those of similar screening on varieties of personality.

Another and certainly more optimistic interpretation would hold that authoritarian students can be somewhat changed as a result of educational practice. At the present time our studies have suggested that these changes are not being accomplished. If one were to assume that shifts could be brought about, then one would need to search for a number of new devices to do it. Perhaps gradually changing class practices from authoritarian to non-authoritarian in approach might allow the rigid person to become less so. Perhaps there are training devices such as those currently being explored for developing creativity which could help students move out of a rigid type of performance. Perhaps the students' own intelligence could be directed toward shifting their patterns of response to a more flexible style.

Before either of these interpretations could be accepted we need to deepen our knowledge considerably. We need to discover to what extent the press of a large, technically oriented land-grant college contributes to more-or-less rigid behavior. We need to discover to what extent such an institution attracts more or fewer students of this type as compared with other types of colleges and universities. We need to discover more of the factors which give rise to this type of person in the first place. And we need to experiment with various ways of coping with him.

At the present time several ideas are being investigated. One teacher in Social Science is going to teach one section of twenty intelligent but rigid students by non-directive means. He is speculating that these students will reject the teaching procedure and will manifest marked hostility toward him and the course. If this proves to be so, then he will seek to modify the students by a number of means and, if this proves impossible, will modify his teaching to meet their expectations.

Another study will be to determine what relationships exist between authoritarianism and critical points in the careers of one class of college students. Warrington (see Chapter 4) has *Inventory of Belief* scores for at least a portion of the group he is considering in his longitudinal study. He plans on studying those scores in relation to the other factors he has accumulated.

Our studies have suggested that personality may be of crucial significance in education. We know that it has not been seriously regarded as a concern of college teachers until recently. We feel it warrants serious and concerted inquiry. But we are talking now of our hopes rather than our accomplishments. Indeed, as we review our work as represented in this volume, we have more of a sense of incompleteness than of accomplishment. This sense of incompleteness makes us hesitant about drawing any overall conclusions. Yet we will record two which are highly subjective, being more the result of experience than of research results. First, we have learned that the desirable quality of continuity in evaluation is difficult to achieve. The follow-through study by Warrington and the drop-out study by Banzet are the only ones that we have been able to maintain for a period exceeding three years. In other cases, changing conditions or personnel resulted in discontinuities which make long-term developments difficult if not impossible to evaluate. The maintenance of such continuing projects in the absence of either special grants or unusual personal devotion is difficult.

Second, we have learned that the feelings of people are more important than data in determining the utility of research results. Teachers are not awaiting the results of research studies in order to modify their practices. Students do not change their views and their study practices because we find them not altogether to our liking. Research which does not initially receive approval and which is not accompanied by a continuing involvement of the prospective consumers not only does not effect changes; it may actually jeopardize desirable change because of the antagonism aroused among individuals who might otherwise have been undisturbed at the same change initiated by their colleagues. For effecting changes, cooperative research involving teachers and evaluators is desirable even though the project may be somewhat less carefully planned and carried out than if done entirely by a research specialist. Often the most valuable results of such cooperative projects come from the lessons learned during the project rather than at its conclusion.

The completion of this volume gives us some satisfaction as a record of our efforts; it gives us even more satisfaction because the time expended on it can now be returned to further evaluation and research activity based on increased insight into the problems. But most of all, our satisfaction arises out of realizing more fully than before that some of the studies reported herein have influenced opinion and pointed the way to a changed and— we think—improved educational program. It is fitting that we end with this observation, for it indicates that, to some extent at least, the real end of evaluation has thereby been achieved.

Note

[1] Marvin D. Solomon, "Studies in Mental Rigidity and the Scientific Method," *Science Education,* October 1952, pp. 240–247.

Index

"A student": myth of, 143; solutions to test questions, 129; studies of, 144

Ability levels, and course sequence, 109

Able students, 199, 201

Academic achievement: and aptitudes, 192; and educational plans, 42; inferior, 86

Academic deficiencies and honors, 58

Academic performance, 184

Academic problems, 180

Academic progress, 56

Accelerates, characteristics of, 162, 164

Accleration, 7, 61, 154; and time of graduation, 161; and time use, 161; for high ability levels, 109; policy, 155, 156; practices, 143; to reduce expenses, 160

ACE Psychological Examination, 103, 108, 109, 110, 183

Activity Check List, 187

Adaptability of students, 233

Administrative access to data, 100

Admissions, 99; of students failing entrance examination, 101; policy unrelated to grading standards, 146; program, 20; standards, 10, 17

Adorno, 229

Advisers, student, 9; and curriculum change, 82

Age of students, 34; and attitudes, 222

Agriculture, 90

Allport-Vernon Study of Values, 225

American ideology, 216

Angell-Troyer Self-Scorer, 132

Arithmetic Proficiency Test, 103

Aspiration index, 190

Attitude scale, 221

Attitudes, student, 214; appraisal of, 215; changes in, 220; continua of, 217; definition of, 215; effects of Basic College on, 225, 227; and goals of general education, 223; measurement of, 216; toward Basic courses, 217; toward comprehensive examinations, 93, 220; toward freshman year, 223; toward MSU, 73; toward specific courses, 224

Attrition: after two years, 54, 55, 56; of counseling clinic students, 56

Atypicality, 63

Authoritarianism, 163, 229, 239

Bakan, 132

Banzet, 56, 65, 76, 80, 240

Basic College, 199, 203, 212, 214, 223; attacks on, 5, 6; Dean of, 192; Evaluation Committee of, 113; examinations in, 116, 157; faculty, training of, 13; organiza- of, 5; standards of, 145

Bible, 226

Biological Science, 5, 119, 203, 204; and acceleration, 158

Bloom and Broder, 202

Borderline applicants, 184

Borderline students, 61

Business and Public Service, 60, 86

C average: and below, 84; as a criterion, 106

Carlin, 15, 21, 31, 232

Census, classification use of, 34

Centrality, of personality, 240

Students: approval of general education, 90; awareness of communication skills, 184; background in Basic courses, 111; description of, 51; geographical origins of, 31, 32; independence of, 233; induction of, 184; probation of, 180; reactions of to special permission, 165
Summer clinics, 185
Superior students, 95, 154
Survey: of graduates, 87, 88; of student opinion, 142

Teaching certificate, student desire for, 60
Teaching methods, 13
Term grades, 109. *See also* Grades
Terminal certificate, 58
Test interpretation inventory, 182
Test of English Usage, 103
Theme rating, 116, 127; form for, 125
Thurstone, 226
Transfer rate, increase of, 80
Transfer students, 49, 52, 67; in longitudinal study, 50
Tutorial system, 171
Two-year program, 77

Uniform ratings, 117
University of California, 229
University of Chicago, 202
Unstructured class, 235

Upperclassmen, 224, 228
Upper schools, 9

Value changes, 225
Variance technique, analysis of, 105
Variation: from orthodox procedure, 233; in standards, 145; in student background, 112; in sub-groups, 57
Verbalized thinking, 128
Veterans, 79; and acceleration, 160, 166
Veterinary medicine, 60
Vocational planning, 23, 43, 91, 180, 188

Warrington, 27, 47, 76, 79, 83, 91, 154, 180, 232, 240
Weekly summaries, 181
Weighting: of speech and theme categories, 121; of wrong responses, 130
Withdrawal, reasons for, 66, 67
Withdrawals and ability levels, 109; and future plans, 72
Women students: attitudes toward examinations, 221; fathers of, 35; residence halls, 160
Work experience, of students, 41
Written and Spoken English (course), 5; and acceleration, 158

"Y" grade, 143